BATTING

Also by Carl Yastrzemski
with Al Hirshberg

Yaz

BATTING

Carl Yastrzemski

with Al Hirshberg

New York • The Viking Press

First published in 1972 by The Viking Press, Inc.
625 Madison Avenue, New York, N.Y. 10022

Published simultaneously in Canada by
The Macmillan Company of Canada Limited

SBN 670-14907-1
Library of Congress catalog card number: 73-151260

Printed in U.S.A.

Photographs by Jerry Buckley

Contents

BATTING

1.

THE BAT

Bats are part of baseball. You can't go up to the plate without one. From the moment you begin to play as a child, you must have something to hit the ball with, even if it's only a broomstick or a piece of wood. As you grow older, you become more sophisticated and swing an actual bat. At the Little League level, bat dimensions are fairly standard. The higher you go from Little League, the more bats vary, the more important their size, and the fussier you will be about them.

To the casual observer almost all bats look alike. Certainly two bats within half an ounce of each other in weight and an inch in length would appear identical. So would bats of different shapes, since the differences are so subtle that only close inspection would show them. But those weight fractions, inch lengths, and slight shape differences are so vital that anyone who wants to learn to hit well must be aware of them.

I pick my bats very carefully, just as all professional ballplayers do. Sometimes you read of one ballplayer trying another's bat, occasionally with such success that he actually changes his own the next year. But at least with good hitters these experi-

3

ments rarely work. A hitter worth his salt knows exactly what he wants in a bat. He can spot fractional differences by swinging it, sometimes even just by picking it up. And those fractional variations in length, weight, and shape can make the difference between a successful hitter and an unsuccessful one.

The first rule in picking out a bat is comfort. When you stand at the plate facing a pitcher who can throw anything from a fast ball to a breaking ball over any part of the plate, you won't hit him if you can't get comfortable. And you won't be comfortable unless you use the right bat—not the right bat for somebody else but for you.

You probably won't learn exactly which that is until you get beyond the high school level. In the meantime, unless you're unusually big for your age, your best bet is to use what I did all through high school and the Babe Ruth League (about the fourteen- to seventeen-year age level). My bat, a Louisville Slugger S2 model, was 34 inches long and weighed 32 ounces. It had a very thin barrel, tapering down to a thinner handle, and it happened to be just right at the time.

This was more the result of luck than brains. My father, a semi-pro ballplayer well into his forties—we were teammates for years around Bridgehampton, Long Island, New York, where I grew up—swung a 34-inch, 32-ounce S2, and we had plenty of them around the house. The S2, although sometimes a little hard to control because it is so light, has such a great whip that it is one of the most popular bats in the big leagues. I know many ballplayers who use them. If I'm not mistaken, there are more S2's around our own Red Sox locker room than anything else. In case you're wondering if big-leaguers use high-school-size bats, I'd better explain right here that neither weight nor length has anything to do with the model number. That's determined by the shape of the bat.

After my first year in pro ball I switched to a K48, heavier than the S2 I had used, with a fatter barrel, tapering rather sharply off to the narrower handle. While I did pretty well with it,

I was never quite satisfied. I changed again when I reached the majors in 1961, this time to the 34-inch Ted Williams model that I still use today. The length, with only a few exceptions, is practically standard in the big leagues.

You would expect a big strong guy like Boog Powell of the Orioles to use a heavier bat than, say, a skinny guy like Bud Harrelson of the Mets, and he does. Powell uses an old Mel Ott model, 35 inches long and weighing 36 ounces. Harrelson uses an old Chuck Klein model, 34 inches long and weighing only 31 ounces. That's one of the lightest bats in the major leagues.

Still, Harrelson's bat isn't appreciably lighter than the one used by the biggest man in the majors, Frank Howard of the Senators. At six feet seven inches and about 260 pounds, Howard uses a surprisingly light bat. He starts the season with one that weighs 34 ounces, then drops back to 33 and ends with a 32-ounce bat, only an ounce heavier than Harrelson's. Most of us use heavier bats at the beginning of the season, tapering off as we go along. I start with a 33-ounce bat and drop to 32½. There are two reasons for this. One is that, as the season progresses, I get tired and find the lighter bat easier to handle. The other is that, after swinging a heavier bat, the light one actually feels lighter than it really is.

The Louisville Slugger people, who make bats, know of only one big leaguer who ever went the other way. When he was playing for the Yankees and other major league clubs, Gene Woodling started light and ended heavy. In the early stages of the season he swung a 36-ounce bat, then changed to 37, and finished with a 38. Woodling always said he felt stronger as he went along, which truly put him in a class by himself. Everybody else feels weaker and more tired.

Oddly enough, one of the lightest men in the majors, Matty Alou, who stands five eight and weighs 155 pounds, uses one of the heaviest bats—40 ounces. This is because Alou, a poor hitter with the Giants, became an outstanding hitter under Harry Walker, who managed the Pirates when Alou was traded to them.

Walker turned Alou into a good hitter by making him slow down
the velocity of his swing. The easiest way to do it was to have
Alou use a heavier bat. Alou, despite several bad years at San
Francisco, led the National League in batting his first year at
Pittsburgh. He finished second twice, is nearly always up in the
.330s, and is one of the few active regulars with a lifetime average
of over .300.

Although Walker hasn't managed the Pirates since the middle
of the 1967 season, his influence was so strong that the whole
team still uses heavier bats than any other club in the majors. A
former National League batting champion himself, Walker, one
of the best hitting coaches in the business, believes in meeting the
ball rather than trying to belt it out of sight. It's easier to meet
the ball with a heavy bat than a light one but harder to hit home
runs. Although they get their share of home runs, the Pirates are
better known for their high averages than their power. This is
Walker's philosophy, and his old ball club still adheres to it two
managers later.

Matty Alou is a typical Harry Walker product—a great hitter
for average but not a power hitter. Actually there's no correlation between the size of the bat and the length of the hit, any
more than there is a correlation between the size of the batter and
the length of the hit. Willie Mays, second only to Babe Ruth as
baseball's all-time home run king, isn't a big man. He stands
only five feet eleven inches and weighs less than 190 pounds.
Henry Aaron, third in the all-time home run race, is an inch
taller than Mays but nearly fifteen pounds lighter.

So, you see, size isn't what makes for power. The power comes
from the whip of the bat, not its weight or its length. Even big
men using heavy bats depend more on the whip than the dimensions. Because of their size they can whip bigger bats around,
sometimes resulting in very long home runs. But as Casey Stengel
used to say, a home run is a home run whether it barely clears
a fence or does it with fifty feet to spare. The only real advantage
to a big man using a heavy bat is that sometimes he might not

hit the ball well and still drive it out of the park.

Guys like that are exceptions, not the general rule. A fellow of average proportions must hit the ball on the nose to get distance. The fact that so many do is proof enough that the whip is what counts. Despite his ordinary size Aaron can hit long drives because of his marvelously strong wrists, very possibly the strongest of any ballplayer who ever lived. Both he and Mays have such quick reflexes that they can wait on a pitch until the last minute and still give it a home run ride.

I'm not a big man—in fact, my dimensions are almost exactly the same as Aaron's—but I hit forty-four home runs in 1967 and have a reputation as a power hitter. Yet I don't swing heavy bats, varying, as I have pointed out, between 32½ and 33 ounces. As a Little Leaguer I used a 33-inch bat, standard length at that level. When you figure that I started Little League at the age of ten, it's amazing how slight my bat changes have been. The bat I use as a major leaguer is only two inches longer than my Little League one was, and I doubt if it's more than three ounces heavier.

Most good hitters use different weight bats under changing conditions. Although I start heavy and finish light, I will sometimes go to a heavy bat to break a slump. But I don't make any hard and fast rules about it. If I'm hitting well, I stick with the same bat no matter what time of the season. If I'm having trouble, I'll experiment with just about everything I do at the plate, including the size of the bat I use. I have pulled out of slumps by going from a heavy bat to a light one, and I've done it the other way around.

Generally it makes more sense to use a heavier bat when you're in a slump. You're not inclined to try to pull everything or overwhip. The heavier bat, not being quite so easy to swing, comes around more slowly, giving you a better chance to make contact with the ball. Doing that is always the first step in fighting a slump.

My favorite bat is a model designated by the Louisville Slugger people as a W215. This is actually a Ted Williams model, with a medium barrel tapering off to a medium handle. Williams used an old Lefty O'Doul model, with a barrel exactly like the original but a handle which Williams devised himself—slightly thicker than O'Doul's. Ted's bat was 35 inches long, and he varied the weights between 32 and 33 ounces. As it happens, I use almost exactly the same bats—including weight and length—that Williams used. I wish I could get exactly the same results that Ted did.

Williams, a much bigger man than I—at his peak he stood six four and weighed about 200 pounds—could have handled as big a bat as anyone but preferred the lighter weight, just as Frank Howard does. Yet there are plenty of big league ballplayers both shorter and lighter than Williams or Howard who dislike any bat under 33½ ounces. But that's what makes the baseball world go round.

The old-time sluggers swung much heavier bats than we do today. The really big guys—fellows like Hank Greenberg and Jimmie Foxx and Rudy York and Hack Wilson, for example—used 38 to 42-ounce bats. Babe Ruth, the greatest slugger of them all, never used anything lighter than 40 ounces and often swung bats far heavier—all the way up to 52 ounces. I'm sure he was the only hitter in history ever to use a 52-ounce bat. There is no record of how often he went that high, but he must have at times because he owned several bats that heavy. Even the average weight of his bats—about 46 ounces—was more than anyone else's heaviest.

But from all I've heard about him, Babe was unique. Besides a keen eye and remarkable reflexes, he had weight and strength, most of which was concentrated on the upper part of his body. He wasn't unusually big by today's standards. He stood six feet two and weighed 215 pounds, but his shoulders, arms, and torso were tremendous, while his legs were skinny. Of course he was long before my time, but I have seen pictures of him swinging, and he handled those huge bats like toothpicks. I imagine Ruth got plenty of home runs on balls he didn't hit squarely, but his bat was so big that when he brought it around fast he could drive a ball into the seats or over the fence just by getting a piece of it.

The oddest bat ever used in the majors was Heinie Groh's, a little third baseman who lasted sixteen years in the majors, starting in 1912. Groh, who had no luck with any sort of conventional bat, devised one known as a "bottle bat." From the top down it was very thick, then abruptly became thin at the handle. Groh stood facing the pitcher, with his feet at the two sides of the batter's box. Somehow or other he could turn and swing at the last minute, although they tell me the bat looked bigger than anyone his size (five feet eight and 150 pounds) could handle. He didn't hit many home runs, but he had four .300 seasons and was one of the best fielders of his time. Nobody else ever used a bat like it, and I don't suppose anyone ever will. I'm told Groh was the most awkward-looking batter in the majors, but he was comfortable, and that was all that counted.

Comfort—as I said before, that's the key to any bat. Too many kids in the age bracket immediately following Little League don't even think of comfort. To them the only thing that counts is the long ball. This is the most common mistake teen-age ballplayers make. They take pride in being able to swing a heavy bat, even if it's so big they have trouble carrying it to the plate. If they only realized that the size of the bat is meaningless, they might become better hitters earlier than they do.

In common with practically all big-leaguers, I have about two dozen bats sent from the Louisville Slugger factory, but I often go a full season without using half of them. As a rule I end up with about six favorite bats. When I'm going well, I use the same one all the time. Bats, of course, don't last forever, so sooner or later I have to change. When the time comes, I make sure I have exactly the same model with exactly the same dimensions as the one I had before.

Some hitters break a lot of bats, some very few. I doubt if I break four a year. A broken bat is sometimes the fault of the hitter, sometimes the pitcher, and sometimes the bat itself. Bats get chipped or pock-marked. Some, like people, gain weight as they get older. Of course the gain isn't very much, but when you're dealing in fractions of ounces, any gain means a change. I can tell when a bat has gained as little as a tenth of an ounce. I get so used to it that I know with just one swing that it has become a trifle heavy. Then I discard it.

Many ballplayers break bats because they crowd the plate. A good hitter who does so will fall away to hit an inside pitch. If he doesn't fall away far enough or fast enough, he'll hit the bat on the handle, a common way to break bats. Pitchers who are always trying to jam a hitter (throwing the ball barely over the inside of the strike zone) cause bats to break that way. Most of the bats I've broken have been partly split without my noticing it. One good whack will finish the job. It's embarrassing to see the broken part of the bat go farther than the ball. It's happened to me, as I guess it's happened to everyone who plays ball long enough. If I broke too many bats, I would suspect I was doing something wrong. A good hitter rarely breaks a bat when he's going well. On the other hand, a poor hitter might break a dozen or more a season.

Although the Louisville Slugger people know the exact dimensions of my bats, I still go to the factory every other year to see for myself. I like to make sure nothing goes wrong. And once in a while I'll pick up a new bat that feels so comfortable I might order a few even if it doesn't conform to my own specifications.

Perhaps it's just superstition, but when I go into a prolonged slump (and I've had some pretty awful ones) I constantly change bats. This really doesn't make a great deal of sense, because I never heard of a bat causing a slump. You go into a slump for one of two reasons—either you're hitting the ball well but right at somebody, or you're hitting poorly. When you're hitting well but in bad luck, it's foolish to change. All you can do is ride the slump out. Sooner or later these well-hit balls will drop in.

But you can't ride out a slump caused by your own failures to hit the ball well. All you can do then is experiment, and part of that is with the bat you use. Maybe there are just so many hits in every bat and yours has run out of hits. There are ballplayers who actually believe that. Sometimes, when things are going especially bad, I'm inclined to believe it myself.

In baseball the bat is the tool of a hitter's trade. Anyone who hopes to become a good hitter must always bear that in mind. He might do everything else right, but if he's swinging the wrong bat—wrong for *him*—he's not going to hit the ball very often or very far.

The wrong bat is the one that makes you feel awkward at the plate. The right bat is the one which gives you that warm, comfortable feeling that no matter what the pitcher throws, you can hit it.

Believe me, it's better to miss a few with the right bat than hit a few with the wrong one. Eventually the wrong one will get you into trouble. And, other things being equal, the right one will get you out of it. If you've got the potential, the right bat might get you into the major leagues or even help make a star of you.

1. *The bat:* Be sure you use the one for *you*, not one used by a favorite player or any other ballplayer you admire.

2.
THE GRIP

There is no standard grip, no rule of thumb by which every hitter can be governed. The only general grip rule I ever heard was a negative one—don't bat cross-handed. But usually you don't have to be a big-leaguer or even a grade school ball-player to know that one. Almost anybody who sees a kid trying to bat cross-handed will correct him, if for no other reason than that it can result in a broken wrist or even a broken arm.

Batting cross-handed is reversing your hands from the way they should be when you grip the bat. There are many variations of grips, but they all add up to the same thing—that if you're a right-handed batter, your right hand must be on top and your left underneath, and if you're a left-handed batter like me, your left hand is on top and your right underneath.

Yet some kids find it natural to bat cross-handed. Those who do are probably batting from the wrong side of the plate. A cross-handed rightie is holding the bat the way a left-hander should, and vice versa. So if you find it easier to bat cross-handed, just step into the opposite batter's box and your hands will be in the proper position.

To my knowledge the only great hitter (with the exception of Frank Frisch) who grew up batting cross-handed was Henry Aaron of the Braves. Henry batted cross-handed all the way through high school in his home town of Mobile, Alabama. Everyone including his coach knew it was wrong, but Henry was such a great hitter even then that when he refused to change, nobody forced him to. How he could hit the ball so hard with that wonderful wrist action and not break his arm was a mystery that will never be solved. Even today I doubt if Aaron could tell you the answer.

He changed only when he turned pro, and then against his will. That was in 1951, when he signed with the Indianapolis Clowns in one of the old Negro leagues. Those leagues flourished when organized baseball banned blacks. But when Branch Rickey broke the color line with Jackie Robinson in 1946, the Negro leagues were doomed because the best black ballplayers naturally went into the organized game. Their own leagues died hard, however, and the Clowns were still going in 1951 when Aaron joined them.

Henry, then seventeen years old, was still batting cross-handed. Even with that glaring fault he was such a remarkable hitter that the Clowns wanted him. The first thing they did was make him hold his hands properly, but it took Aaron nearly a year to get used to the idea. Right up to the time he was sold to the Braves' farm chain he sometimes crossed his hands at the plate when he thought nobody was looking. For years after that I'm sure he was tempted. He's probably the only man in baseball history who had hopes of becoming a star batting cross-handed.

But of course this would have been impossible. Aaron became great only by learning to hold his hands properly on the bat. And when I say "properly," I don't mean in any particular manner —only that he learned to place his hands in the correct order for a right-handed batter.

To me the most important thing for a young ballplayer to do is choke his bat, even if it's only half an inch. When you hear the expression "swing from the heels," you visualize the hitter holding the bat at the very end. Actually nearly all hitters, even big strong sluggers, choke their bats a little. I know of very few major leaguers who rest their lower hand on the knob of the bat.

Just how high you should choke the bat is something you must find out for yourself. Before I learned a few of the tricks of actually going for home runs from Ted Williams, when he was a Red Sox spring-training batting coach, I choked my bat more than I do now. As a matter of fact, pictures of me swinging seem to show that I don't choke it at all, but this is an optical illusion. I'll admit I don't choke it much—perhaps a quarter of an inch—but I choke it.

I go higher when in a slump. Obviously the more you choke, the better your control of the bat. You can, of course, choke too much. Sometimes a ballplayer chokes his bat so high that he can't get the fat of it on anything over the outside corner of the plate. But this is a rare fault in the majors, and hardly a fault at all in a boy at the Little League or high school level.

In learning to grip the bat properly you must bear in mind only a few general rules. Otherwise, as in picking out a bat, the choice is yours. However, the rule of comfort doesn't apply, as in selecting a bat. This is because a proper grip usually must be acquired. Very few boys naturally hold their bats properly. Witness Henry Aaron. He was most comfortable holding the bat the wrong way. To make it to the majors he *had* to change.

So did I. If I held the bat today as I did as a kid, I would have been lucky to make it to a Class A league. Up to my high school days I was a bunter and a spray hitter because I tried to grip the bat like a slugger, which I wasn't built for. Like every other kid, I wanted to hit home runs. I tried an interlocking grip, with the thumb of one hand curled around the little finger of the other, as a golfer does. This is sometimes effective for big strong guys because you get maximum power that way, but not for others.

I soon discovered it wasn't for me. I just didn't have the strength to control the bat. Then I decided to settle for bunts and spray hits. I changed my grip, interlocking my fingers but holding my hands so that the knuckles of each weren't lined up. I controlled the bat with my left or upper hand, using my right for leverage. When I stood at the plate and looked down at my hands, I could see my left knuckles in one direction and my right in another. This is not bad for a short hitter, and in fact I had astronomical batting averages that didn't mean anything. One year I think I hit over .600 during a grade school season, with most of the hits bunts or bleeders or beaten-out nubbers that didn't roll as far as the pitcher's box.

My dad helped me out of that situation. He made me grip the bat with my knuckles lined up evenly, so that when I looked down, all I could see beneath my upper thumb was the knuckle of my left forefinger. This is not an easy way to hold the bat, but if you can get used to it, it's effective in generating power.

Pick up a bat. Without knowing anything about grips, just hold it as if you were about to swing it. Then look at your knuckles. I'll bet you won't have them lined up evenly. That's the natural way to hold a bat, but not the best way—not if you want both control and power. You will have control, but when you swing you'll be wasting power.

To switch from the way I had been holding the bat to the way I hold it now was a tough job which took me two years. But once I learned the trick, I was on my way toward being both a good hitter and a long-ball hitter. I have seen my dad, smaller than I am since I reached maturity, hit some tremendous shots. By nature and build he was a line-drive or spray hitter. But by holding the bat with his knuckles lined up evenly, he could hit occasional home runs. He couldn't have done it without that type of grip.

The big advantage to it is that you get the best wrist action this way. Most good hitters are wrist hitters, as are many sluggers. Look at Aaron and Mays, if you want the most obvious examples. Both hold their bats with the knuckles of both hands in line. Yet even that isn't a hard and fast rule. The grip is flexible. Lots of

long hitters do very well without lining up their knuckles, but
most of them don't depend as heavily on wrist as on shoulder
or body action.

When you first stand at the plate waiting for the ball to leave
the pitcher's hand, hold your bat loosely enough so that your
hands feel relaxed. If you don't, you're likely to leave your hits
in the batter's box. Don't tighten your grip until you are ready
to swing. Then, especially if you are a strong hitter, you must
hold the bat as tightly as possible so that it won't wobble and
change its angle as you bring it around.

I have seen guys hold a bat so loosely that anyone could come
up behind them and knock it out of their hands. Hawk Harrelson, who played for the Red Sox for a season and a half, almost
lets the bat fall while waiting for a pitch. But when it leaves the
pitcher's hand, Harrelson has such a firm grip that his control
of the bat is perfect as he swings.

The loosest grip I ever heard of was Gil McDougald's when he
first came up to the Yankees. McDougald retired the year before
I joined the Red Sox, and by that time he had long since changed
his grip—largely, I'm told, because it drove Manager Casey
Stengel crazy. As a rookie McDougald held the bat so loosely
that he almost dragged it in the dirt behind him. It gave Stengel
the heebie-jeebies to watch him. Casey couldn't figure how it was
possible for a man to bring his bat up and grip it hard as
quickly as McDougald did, and neither could anyone else. I
don't know whether the change helped McDougald or not. It
certainly didn't hurt him because he was a fine hitter all through
his career. Still, I often wondered why Stengel, after spending
several years as a Giants' teammate of Heine Groh's, should
worry about an unorthodox grip as long as the guy who used it
could hit the ball.

Some ballplayers run their hands up and down the handle to
make sure they remain loose and relaxed until the time comes
for their actual swing. The two most prominent I can think of
offhand are Ralph Kiner and Ernie Banks. Kiner led the National

League in home runs seven years in a row, and Banks is one of baseball's all-time stars, so their system obviously works.

I couldn't do that because I'd be afraid of losing control of the bat. I hold mine rather loosely, but keep my hands in one place. I pump quite a lot and often step in and out of the batter's box. While waiting for the pitch, my grip on the bat is just strong enough to keep it high and away from my shoulder. I tighten as the ball approaches me, and by the time I swing I have a firm hold on the bat.

Just to show you how hard it is to set any rules on gripping the bat, let me say right here that one of the greatest hitters of all time, Ted Williams, had such a tight grip on the bat while standing at the plate that his knuckles went white. But Williams, as in so many other ways, was a classic exception. Anyone who can pile up a lifetime average of .344 in twenty-two years in the majors certainly didn't leave many hits in the batter's box.

One of the most common faults of young hitters is holding the bat with the fingers. The handle should rest in the palms of your hands so that the fingers are free to control the wrist snap as you swing. The best way to learn how to use your palms when holding the bat is to spread your fingers wide after you pick it up. Once it is firm enough in the palms to keep from falling, you wrap your fingers around it. Of course your fingers will be on the bat, but the pressure that holds it is basically in your hands. The only analogy I can think of—and it's a long way from baseball— is the way a violinist holds his instrument. As you watch, he seems to be holding it with the hand down at the narrow end. Actually he holds it with his chin, leaving his fingers free to manipulate the strings. If he takes that hand off, the violin won't drop. And if you release all your fingers, your bat, although it might be wobbly, shouldn't drop either.

Almost everyone holds his hands together with the little finger of one touching the thumb of the other. This isn't just for maximum power, although it's pretty hard to get that with your hands apart. But keeping them together makes for a more rhythmic swing and helps you give your wrist that snap it needs as you bring your bat around.

The only guy I've ever seen bat with his hands apart (except in bunting) was Mike Andrews, and he did it because he had to. In 1969, while with our club, he suffered a hand injury that seemed minor but turned out to be bad enough to keep him on the bench five weeks. While doctors experimented and Andrews climbed the walls in frustration, the swelling and pain hung on and on. When Mike finally got back into the line-up, his hand, though healing, still wasn't right. It hurt every time he swung, so he tried holding it away from the other hand. He batted two weeks that way. Although he didn't do badly, he was very happy when the hand healed enough for him to go back into his regular swing.

As always, there have been notable exceptions to the rule of keeping your hands together. Two of the greatest hitters who ever lived, Ty Cobb and Honus Wagner, batted with their hands apart. Both of course were several generations ahead of me, and I never saw either. How they could do so well with such an unorthodox grip (they held the bat almost identically) only they will ever know. However, Wagner spent all his career and Cobb most of his in the era of the dead ball.

When Babe Ruth changed the whole philosophy of baseball with his home run hitting, the game's powers-that-be livened up the ball in the early twenties. At that point, I'm told, Cobb, who some claim was the greatest hitter of all time, brought his hands together occasionally, just to prove he could hit for power. When he was over forty, he hit three homers in one game, and to the day of his death he claimed he could have done as well as anyone in the power department if he wanted to. But right up to the end of his career he batted with his hands apart.

I'd like to see somebody try that today. Although it would keep a guy from hitting many home runs, I imagine it would give him the best bat control possible. I'm sure it would help a small man who could never expect to be more than a spray hitter or a place hitter, but I wouldn't recommend it to anyone else.

Speaking of holding your hands apart, the one time you must do this is when you're bunting. I have heard power hitters (including myself) criticized for not bunting enough, but what would be the point? If a man has the potential to hit the ball out of the park, why waste him as a bunter? On the other hand, every hitter must know how to bunt, because you never know when a bunting situation will come up which might include even a long-ball hitter.

We all practice bunting, even those of us who rarely bunt in a ball game. It is an art which requires a specific style. Pitchers and weak hitters—the men most likely to bunt—usually know best how to do it because they practice it the most. In bunting, the batter applies no power whatever, letting the pitcher supply that. You should stand at the plate in your normal hitting position, then square away to bunt *after* the ball leaves the pitcher's hand.

"Squaring away" simply means facing the pitcher, your bat parallel to the ground, with one hand near the handle and the other near the label. Your only job is to let the ball hit the bat, making sure you don't hit under the pitch so that you won't pop up. Since the normal function of a bunt is to sacrifice a man on base along, a pop-up can be a disaster that results in a sure double play because the man on base is often running with the pitch. And since you're most likely to pop up on a high pitch, that's what you'll get in a bunting situation.

There are actually two kinds of bunts—one to sacrifice and one to get on base. The sacrifice bunt is obvious to everyone in the ball park. The other kind, usually a "drag" bunt, depends heavily on the surprise element for success. It's most successful with the bases empty and the fielders all in their regular positions back near the outfield grass.

Sometimes even a power hitter will bunt if the situation is right. With the infield back and neither the pitcher nor the catcher expecting it, I have bunted just to get on base in a close game. I bat third, and with a good cleanup man like Reggie Smith behind me, there is always a chance that he will hit behind me so that I can go from first to third. However, I won't bunt often—maybe half a dozen times a season—and I don't recall getting orders to lay down a sacrifice bunt in years.

The best bunter of modern times was Phil Rizzuto, now a Yankees radio and television announcer. Rizzuto once helped the Yankees clinch a pennant with a surprise bunt in Boston. The bases were full with two out in the ninth inning of a tie game when Rizzuto came to the plate. Under those conditions a bunt is the very last thing you would expect. With a play at every base the Red Sox infielders were deep. Rizzuto caught everybody including the pitcher flat-footed when he bunted between first base and the mound. By the time anyone had caught up with the ball, the winning run had scored and Rizzuto was on.

In 1946 Ted Williams, playing in his only World Series, had a sore elbow, the result of having been hit by a pitched ball a few days before the series began. The Cardinals, like most teams who played the Red Sox in those days, used a radical shift on the left-handed Williams, with the fielders packed on the right side and practically nobody protecting the left. Williams had five hits in that series, all singles. One was a bunt down the third base line.

The Dodgers always played Henry Aaron deep, even in bunt situations. One night, with Jackie Robinson playing third base, Aaron laid down a bunt toward third and was across first base before Robinson had the ball in his hand. Later Aaron said to Robinson, "You keep playing me that way, and I'll get a sure single every time I bunt."

"You're welcome to it," Robinson replied. "We'll give you a bunt single every time over a possible home run."

When I'm in a slump, I wish third basemen would treat me that way. I'd bunt until the cows came home.

2. *The grip:* This and the pictures that follow show the correct sequence in gripping the bat.

3. Left hand first, or right hand first if you are a right-handed batter.

4. Note the slight choking of the bat.

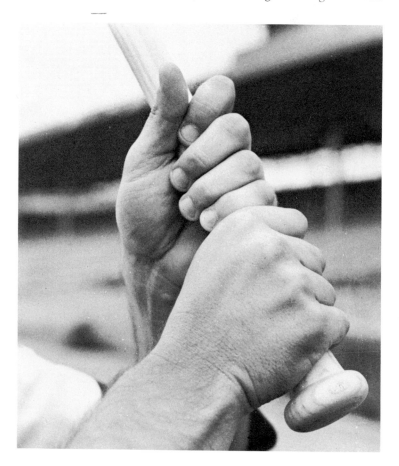

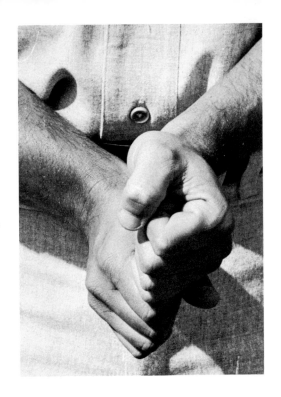

5. Little finger of left hand touching thumb of right. Vice versa for a right-handed batter.

6. Front view.

3.
THE STANCE

Nothing characterizes a batter's style more obviously than his stance. To fans, bats and grips look pretty much alike because their differences are too subtle to be noticed from a distance. But a ballplayer's stance is his trade-mark, the one thing he does at the plate that can be seen and analyzed from as far away as the center field bleachers.

Like the bat, the stance is variable, with comfort the keynote. There are almost as many different stances as there are big league ballplayers. Each man has his own way of covering the plate, the one thing that must be done by every successful hitter. No matter how you stand, you must be in a position to get the fat of your bat on the pitch that counts—either the two-strike pitch that's in the strike zone or the pitch you find easiest to hit.

Just as everyone who steps to the plate has his weaknesses, every good professional ballplayer has his strengths. It doesn't take long for pitchers to find out these things. I never saw a major league hitter with a fundamental weakness the opposition didn't know about. On the other hand, I have seen a ballplayer sometimes kill a pitch that's supposed to be one that ordinarily gives him trouble.

Naturally I keep going back to 1967 because that was my big year. While the Red Sox were winning the pennant, I won the American League's Triple Crown, leading the league in batting and runs batted in and tying with Harmon Killebrew of the Twins for the home run leadership. In the last two months of that season I guess I couldn't do anything wrong. The pitchers gave me good balls to hit, even when they threw to my presumed weakness— low, inside, and over the strike zone. I hit more than one homer on pitches like that.

Most hitters have trouble when pitchers try to jam them—that is, throw the ball on the inside part of the strike zone near the wrist. Some guys never learn how to handle a jamming situation. Some try to bail out—step a little into the bucket—in order to hit the ball on the fat of the bat rather than on the handle.

However, a good hitter can see he is being jammed as he watches the flight of the ball after it leaves the pitcher's hand. When I see the pitch coming, I step forward soon enough to try to hit the ball before it reaches the plate. When I'm in my groove and not slumping, that works pretty well. Since the pitchers know that, they don't often try to jam me except when my bat is ice-cold. Then it doesn't matter—I can't hit anything until I regain my normal bat control.

There are hitters who change their stances to compensate for certain factors—whether the pitcher's strength is a fast ball or a breaking pitch, whether or not he likes to jam you, or whether or not you, as the hitter, are trying to outguess him. I rarely change my stance from one time at bat to the next. Normally I'm almost a straight-up hitter, with my feet fairly wide apart, my bat high, my elbows away from my body, my shoulder tucked in, my knees slightly bent.

When I'm hitting the ball and not experimenting while trying to break a slump, I stand that way against all but two American League pitchers. The only men who make me change my stance are knuckle-ball pitchers—Hoyt Wilhelm, who is no longer in the league, and Wilbur Wood. Both are standouts, and it's generally accepted that neither is sure where the ball will go. I find this very hard to believe. I can't speak for any other hitter, but when Wilhelm faced me, his knuckler broke down and inside, so I moved farther away from the plate. I stand closer than usual against Wood because his knuckler breaks down and away from me.

But my normal stance, while not the classic one, is similar to it. Yes, there is a classic stance—the picture-book look, which sometimes works and sometimes doesn't. There's no way of teaching anyone exactly how to stand. The big thing is to cover all parts of the strike zone. If a man can do that comfortably without hurting his swing, it doesn't matter much how he stands. On the other hand, the few great hitters who use the classic stance are wonderful to see in action. Unfortunately a lot of guys who try it don't hit well from it. Eventually they either change or go out of business. Looking good at the plate doesn't mean anything unless you can hit the ball.

Joe DiMaggio was the perfect combination, for his was the classic stance and no one ever took better advantage of it. Besides being one of the greatest hitters of all time, he was one of the most beautiful to watch. He stood with his bat high, his feet wide apart, his knees slightly bent. While not on top of the plate like Frank Robinson or Tony Conigliaro, for example, he was still close enough to cover the entire strike zone. When he took his short stride and brought his bat around in that smooth arc, he was truly poetry in motion.

Ted Williams' stance wasn't classic, but very close to it. Williams' feet were wide apart, but I don't think he held his bat as high as DiMaggio did. When DiMaggio stood at the plate, he broke no conventional batting rules. Williams broke two. He held his bat in a death grip simply standing there, whereas most hitters hold theirs loosely until the last minute. And Williams had a bad hitch in his swing—suicide for anyone else but perfect for him.

A hitch is something in your swing that isn't normal. Either you drop your hands or raise them just before you start your swing. Every other hitter I have ever seen or heard of (including myself) would be in serious trouble with a hitch like Williams', for whichever way your hands go as you start the swing, you must bring them back to a normal position before you can make contact with the ball. This is an extra move which complicates the problem of hitting, and heaven knows there are complications enough in the normal course of events.

Unlike everyone else, Williams, who dropped his hands, never raised them back, and actually swung from his hitch. I never heard of another hitter who could do that. Ordinarily a hitch not only wrecks your timing but gets you out of your normal groove and changes the arc of your swing. Aside from everything else, it makes you move your head, which is as suicidal in baseball as in golf. You must keep your head steady so you don't take your eyes off the ball. Almost anyone else with a hitch falls into all those traps, but Williams' hitch was part of his swing.

Although I never discussed it with him, I think the reason for his hitch was his own conviction that a batter should hit slightly under the ball. This was in direct contrast to Bobby Doerr's theory. When Doerr was the Red Sox batting coach under Manager Dick Williams, he always said you should hit slightly over the ball. Both former Red Sox stars have had great success as hitting teachers, so maybe there's something in what each says. When I'm at the plate, I stand in a way that seems best for me to hit the ball squarely.

There was one other unusual feature of Williams' stance. Once in the batter's box, he never moved his back foot. No matter how close the ball came at him, he simply moved his head or his shoulders or his front (right) foot to get out of the way, but that back foot always remained anchored. I never played on the same Red Sox team with him, but they tell me pitchers almost never tried to knock him down. In the days when they did—and he had to move his back foot when he hit the dirt—he often belted the next pitch out of sight.

In most cases (though not all) the best general rule is to take a stance that will cause as little unnecessary movement as possible. Every move you make at the plate as you prepare to swing is another invitation for a costly mistake. That's why most of the best hitters spread their legs at least as far apart as I do. The farther apart your legs, the shorter your stride. Although I'm sure there have been good hitters who stood with their legs close together, I have never seen a great one do that, and I doubt if there have been very many in the whole history of major league baseball.

Ty Cobb was one of the few, but he was in a class by himself because he constantly changed his stance, batting differently against different pitchers. He hit with his feet sometimes close together and sometimes apart. But Cobb apparently was comfortable in any one of a dozen stances. Ordinary mortals like myself must use the same general stance all the time or they ask for trouble.

Stan Musial was another great hitter who kept his legs pretty close together. He batted from a crouch, uncoiling himself like a steel spring as he brought his bat around. That was great for him, but I would not advise it for anyone else with hitting ambitions. If he hadn't been such a marvelous hitter from the start, a good batting coach would long ago have tried to straighten him up and make him spread out more.

But for some reason or other we all have a tendency to go into something of a crouch without realizing it. I remember in my early days with the Red Sox when Ted Williams, who had retired but was still a spring-training batting coach, came to Boston at owner Tom Yawkey's request to try to break me out of a dismal slump.

Williams wouldn't let me go to the plate before sitting in the dugout talking with me for about fifteen minutes. It was on the morning of a night game, and the only people around were Joe Coleman, Sr. (whose son Joe later pitched for Williams when Ted managed the Washington Senators); Rudy York, then the

Red Sox batting coach; Sal Maglie, the pitching coach; a few kids to shag in the outfield; and Yawkey, who leaned against the low wall in front of the box seats near the Red Sox dugout. Coleman, a former big league pitcher himself, lived in a Boston suburb and often pitched batting practice for the Red Sox.

After finishing our talk in the dugout, Williams said, "O.K., now let's see you hit."

While he stood behind the batting net, I went to the plate. The moment I took my stance, Williams yelled, "Why the big crouch?"

"Crouch?" I said. "Am I in a crouch?"

"That's probably your whole trouble," Williams said. "Straighten up."

I straightened up, and after an hour of work was hitting the ball well. That night I got a couple of hits.

You might ask, if the crouch was so obvious that Williams could spot it, why couldn't it have been spotted by somebody on the ball club? The answer is, the crouch was not that pronounced. When you see a man at bat every day, it's very hard to notice anything different about his stance, unless the difference is radical. Actually, few of us ever do anything very different from normal once we have developed our regular habits. My change into a crouch wasn't something that had happened overnight, but over a period of weeks. Although Williams had called it a "big crouch," it was really a very slight one. It just looked big to Williams, who hadn't seen me since spring training.

You might also ask why even a slight crouch should make such a difference in my batting average. That is simply another example of the old adage that baseball is a game of inches—or fractions of inches. Slight as it was, my crouch was just enough to get me out of my groove. Not realizing I was in a crouch, I didn't try to correct it, with the result that I was hitting too far under the ball, which caused me to pop up a lot.

While a pronounced crouch was not for me—nor for most hitters who have the power, timing, and reflexes to knock the ball out of the park—it does have its advantages. A small man who doesn't figure to hit many home runs is often better off batting from a crouch than he would be standing straight up. His size alone gives him a smaller strike zone and the pitcher a tougher target. By going into a crouch—as, for example, Eddie Stanky did—he makes his own strike zone even smaller.

They didn't call Stanky "the walking man" for nothing. He got more passes for a hitter of limited ability than any ballplayer of modern times. A little guy to start with, he could shrink the pitcher's target down to almost zero by crouching. Although a pitcher could keep him from hitting the long ball, it was no cinch getting him out. He did get his share of hits for a man his size. But his job was to get on base, and a pass was as good as a single for him. He got millions of them.

Only two kinds of ballplayers get lots of passes—sluggers with a big home run potential and small men who know how to take advantage of their size. I would advise any small man (under five nine) to bat from a crouch. Most who make it to the majors do. And I don't mind telling you they drive pitchers nuts.

In general it makes sense to stand as close to the plate as possible, if only to keep it covered. Everyone has his own way of covering his strike zone. Mine, as I have mentioned, is simply to reach out with my bat to make sure I can touch the other side of the plate without moving my feet. But that's no more a hard and fast rule than most other statements about a stance.

Some men stand so deep in the batter's box that they can't possibly touch the other side of the plate with their bats. Rogers Hornsby, one of the greatest hitters of all time, stood so far away from the plate that no one saw how he could ever get the fat of his bat on a pitch on the outside corner. For years pitchers threw the ball away from him, but he still creamed it. They tell me he was one of the few great all-time hitters without a weakness. He himself always said the toughest pitch for a good hitter was inside and across the letters, but he could belt those as well as anything else.

I know of several National Leaguers who did pretty well from deep in the box—Eddie Mathews, Gordon Coleman, and Earl Torgeson, for example. But while they all kept the back foot deep, they were close to the line with the front foot, stood with their legs well apart, and could get their hits by taking a short stride.

One of the most famous stances in baseball history was Mel Ott's. He must have been one of the shortest sluggers of all time—he was just five feet nine and weighed about 170. But he ended up with 511 home runs, which stood for years as a National League record until Willie Mays broke it. Ott, who batted left-handed, had an odd way of lifting his front foot as he began his swing—a habit that would ruin most hitters. But he came down just in time to be in perfect balance when he actually made contact with the ball, I've seen a few others do what Ott did, but none with much success.

The modern ballplayer nearest to Ott is Dick McAuliffe of the Tigers. Also a left-handed hitter, McAuliffe lifts his right foot fairly high just before he swings, then comes down in time to keep himself evenly balanced as he brings his bat around. Although he gets occasional home runs, McAuliffe is more dangerous as a line-drive and slap hitter than as a slugger. Yet his peculiarity at the plate is, I'm told, very close to Ott's.

Another fine hitter with an unusual stance is Hawk Harrelson of the Indians, who was with us for part of 1967, all of 1968, and the beginning of the 1969 season. His best year was 1968, when he led the league in runs batted in and was named the American League's Player of the Year.

The looseness with which he holds his bat is one of two distinctive features of his stance. The other is the way he stands. While his back foot (his right, for he bats right) is squarely planted in the batter's box, he lets only the toe of his left foot touch the ground. This doesn't affect his stride at all. When he's ready to swing, he just steps forward and is well balanced at the time he hits the ball.

In the many hours I've spent with Hawk in batting practice—

though one of the game's most offbeat characters, he works as hard on the field as any ballplayer I know, and takes far more batting practice than most guys—he never could explain to me the reason for his stance. All he ever said when I asked him was, "It's just more comfortable." Of course he meant that it was more comfortable for *him*. For anyone else it would be awkward.

Babe Ruth, the greatest slugger of all time, had one of the most unusual stances of all time. He stood with his back almost facing the pitcher, so that in order to watch him the Babe had to peek over his shoulder. His feet were close together, the back foot firm but the front one similar to Harrelson's, with only the toe touching the ground. I doubt if anyone else in major league history could get by with a stance like that, because the Babe had an awful lot of unwinding to do while bringing his bat around. On top of that he had to take a very long stride, much as Musial did. How Ruth hit the ball at all is still a mystery to batters who have seen movies of him in action. It always looked to me as if he would have a terrible time getting into a good position to swing, but he never did.

Which brings me to another important point in the stance—don't copy your favorite ballplayer. I imagine dozens of kids must have ruined their chances of becoming good hitters by trying to imitate Babe Ruth. Too many young ballplayers still make the mistake of copying the stance of a personal favorite. Anyone who tried Ott's method or Musial's or McAuliffe's or Harrelson's, for example, would be in trouble from the start.

Don't try to copy anyone—even the great sluggers. You won't get good results unless his style happens to be exactly the one that suits you best—and that's highly unlikely. You must develop your own stance and change it only as it suits *you*. You can watch a Williams or a DiMaggio or a Musial or a Mays or an Aaron from now until doomsday, but the odds are against you if you try to copy any of them.

I might include myself in that category. Don't forget—I changed my own stance after I reached the majors. That in itself is pretty unusual. By the time a youth reaches the majors his stance should be pretty well set. I know of few other ballplayers who changed as late as I did, although I know plenty who have experimented with other stances. They almost always go back to the one they came up with, although there have been a few exceptions.

When I first turned pro, I stood with my feet closer together than I do now, and I didn't hold my bat nearly as high. Later, after I reached the majors, they made me spread out more and hold my bat high because I had a tendency to keep my elbow too close to my body. It worked well enough, but to this day I sometimes catch myself holding my bat too high. That makes me have to bring it down too fast, and more than once this tendency has started slumps.

One of the greatest hitters who ever lived, Shoeless Joe Jackson, stood with his feet so close together that he had to take a tremendous stride. Unfortunately Jackson, as one of the "Black Sox" who threw the 1919 World Series to the Reds, never got full credit for his ability because of his part in that baseball scandal. But men who saw him tell me he was an absolute marvel. He hit the dead ball with power, and if he had played a few more years, he might have given even the peerless Ruth a run for his money as a home run hitter.

While it is normally inadvisable to move around too much at the plate, two of the best hitters in baseball, Frank Howard and Tony Oliva, are almost never still. Howard pumps his bat constantly, a habit most of us have to some degree. When Ted Williams became the Senators' manager, he tried to stop Howard from pumping so much, but Howard still does it more than most big-leaguers. It certainly hasn't hurt his hitting. In 1969, his first year under Williams, he had the best season of his life.

Oliva not only pumps but also wiggles all over the place. As he stands at the plate, he moves everything—bat, feet, arms, hips, head, everything. I doubt if anyone else could do all the things Oliva does and be anywhere near the hitter he is. If you saw a kid breaking into the pros with all Oliva's movements, you'd tell him he'd never get beyond Class A ball if he didn't stop. Maybe somewhere down the line, managers and coaches tried to stop Oliva, but they never succeeded. It didn't matter, of course. Oliva is as fine a hitter as there is in the majors. Wiggling and pumping and jumping all over the place are all just part of his batting style.

One of the best of the present-day Yankees is Bobby Murcer, who bats from a pronounced crouch. Murcer is not a great hitter, but he's all big-leaguer both on the field and at the plate. I don't know if anyone ever tried to straighten him up, but he hits well enough from his crouch, and it would do him more harm than good to change now.

All of which is more important in what it doesn't prove than in what it does. For when you study batting stances, you can't logically make up any set rules about them. It truly makes no difference how a man stands at the plate as long as he covers the right territory—the strike zone. Unless the way he stands obviously keeps him from hitting the ball, the best thing to do—if he can hit—is to leave him alone. There was an old story about Ted Williams asking the late Lefty O'Doul, a two-time big league batting champion, what he should do to become a better hitter.

"Don't do anything," O'Doul said. "You're perfect just the way you are."

Which of course was true. Williams probably knew more about hitting the day he was born than most other guys learn in a lifetime.

7. and 8. *The stance:* Bat high, shoulders in, chin tucked into shoulder.

9. Position of legs.

10. Position of hips—
slight crouch.

11. Rear view. Bat high, chin tucked in, legs apart, shoulder in close.

12. Note waist, shoulders, head, position of bat.

13. Front view.

14. and 15. Waiting for pitch.

16. View from behind catcher and umpire.

17. Close-up of head, hands and shoulders.

18. Front close-up from waist up.

19. Close-up of head and grip.

20. Eyes on pitcher, then on ball.

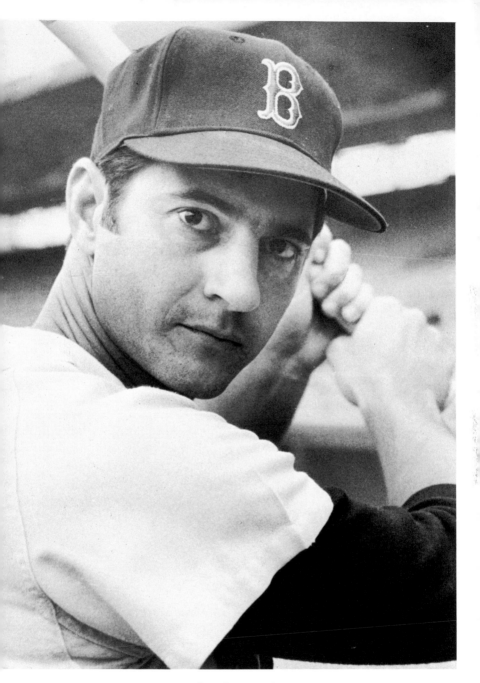

21. Another close-up of eyes.

22. Position of waist and hi

23. Close-up of legs.

4.

THE SWING

$\mathbf{Y}$ou often hear the expression, "He has a nice, smooth, level swing." Forget the "level" part. No good hitter ever swings level—that is, parallel to the ground. You either swing a little bit up or a little bit down. Otherwise your swing would be hopelessly awkward. And if your natural swing is level, forget baseball unless you're a pitcher.

They ought to throw that word "level" out of all batting vocabularies. If you try to swing level, your shoulders and elbows won't function properly. Your shoulders will carry your whole body around and your elbows will stick out like the ears of a loving cup. You will hit the ball only by sheer luck because by trying to swing level to the ground you'll lose control of your bat.

As I say, every good hitter swings either down or up. I'm an uppercut hitter. I try to hit just a trifle below the center of the ball as it comes in. If I make good contact, the ball will go up in the air, and if I'm lucky it will go out of the park. This happens to be my style, as it is the style of some other hitters, but that doesn't mean it's the only way to get the ball into the air.

Rico Petrocelli of our club broke the record for home runs by a shortstop when he hit forty in 1969. He chops down on the ball. In other words he tries to hit it a little above the center. When he makes the best contact, he hits the ball out as well, although his home runs usually travel in a slightly different arc from mine.

Petrocelli is about my height, but I'm sure his shoulders and the upper part of his body are stronger. We both hit a lot of line drives, but mine seldom go out of the park, while many of his do. I've hit a few long screamers in my time, but Rico has hit dozens.

Tony Oliva of the Twins, one of the best hitters in the business, is an uppercutter like me and gets at least as good results as I do —usually better. When he makes the right contact, his hit goes like a shot. Whether it's for distance or not—even if it's a sizzler right at somebody—it's effective.

Ted Williams—I guess I'll always go back to Ted Williams because the guy was so great at the plate—was an uppercut hitter who belted truly awesome line drives. He probably lost ten or fifteen points off his lifetime batting average (.344) because of the radical shift opposing teams used on him. Everyone played him to pull the ball, with all but a couple of men covering the right side of the diamond. Not until late in his career did Williams start poking the ball to left to keep the opposition honest. In the meantime he hit scores of murderous line drives that were caught by the second baseman or even the shortstop playing a short right field, an area that is a sure hit against a normal alignment.

A good natural swing is something that really can't be taught. You have to be born with it, then nurture it as you grow up by swinging and swinging and swinging until you can't lift your arms any more. Nothing takes more practice than the swing. Each man has his own groove, and no matter how much alike two hitters may look to the casual fan, each man has his own swing.

Of course there are always similarities between hitters. For example, Al Kaline of the Tigers and I have much the same swing. From the stands we may even look alike, but we're not. There are subtle differences between us because there are subtle differences between all hitters.

I once heard a batting coach in a locker room say, "There are twenty-five different men in this room and no two of them swing alike." He might have added, "There are six hundred ballplayers in the big leagues and no two of *them* swing alike."

Yet the pay-off in hitting is the swing. The boy who has a good swing can grow up into the man who is a major league star. The boy with an awkward swing or a basically unnatural one will have to make it in the majors as a pitcher because he'll never make it as a hitter. There are a few exceptions like Heinie Groh, to whom I referred in an earlier chapter, but very few indeed.

This is one way a good big league scout can tell if a boy might ever become a big league hitter. The swing is the first thing the scout looks at. Even if the boy doesn't make contact—even if he's a poor hitter when the scout sees him—he has a chance to make the grade if his swing is smooth and natural. Many a good big league hitter today was a bad one in high school. Obviously he made plenty of mistakes as a kid, but he had the swing. With that for a start he *can* be taught.

But he must work his brains out, and I mean that almost literally. For the day will come—if he makes it—when his brain works so fast telling his arms when to swing that the swing will be automatic. He develops his hitting ability with practice as he grows up. That's when he does all the thinking about his swing. After he reaches the majors, he has plenty of time to think of other fundamentals such as his bat, his grip, his stance, and all the million and one things every hitter must think about, but the one thing he should never have to think about is his swing.

That is, of course, if he's hitting the ball. If he isn't, then perhaps he must think of the swing because he might be out of his groove. The Red Sox take movies of every ballplayer when he is hitting well. If he goes into a slump, the first place he runs to is the projection room to see what he might be doing differently from when he *was* hitting.

The difference may be minor and easy to correct. He may be standing a little too far in one direction or another, or holding his bat too high, or taking his eye off the ball, or not tucking his shoulders in, or striding wrong. Corrections or adjustments can easily be made under these conditions. But if his problem is his swing, he's in trouble. Then he has to start thinking of something that he was born with and that has become second nature to him.

It's like a beginner taking golf lessons. The pro says, "Keep your head down; keep your right knee and left elbow stiff; spread your legs; make sure the club is in the right position." As long as he is learning, he must consciously think of all those things. But once he learns—if he ever does—everything is automatic. When he reaches that stage, all he has to worry about are the refinements. But when his swing goes sour again, he's in trouble.

It's the same in baseball. If you start having trouble with your swing, you've got a tough job ahead of you to make it right because your brain must work overtime. It can't signal your arms fast enough to swing. In golf that's really not so bad. You can stand over a golf ball all day before swinging and you won't be hurt. But you can't stand at the plate all day, because the pitcher isn't going to wait for your arms to get the message from your brain that it's time to swing.

I've seen many a potentially great hitter go right out of business because his swing gets fouled up and he can't correct it. He has one great year or maybe even two, then suddenly fades into oblivion. A patient manager or club owner may keep him around two or three years simply because it's hard to believe that he has lost that great swing which made him look so good starting out.

On the other hand, I've seen hitters traded who looked as if they would never regain their swings, and who then suddenly exploded. This happened to Frank Howard, who always gave promise after signing for a big bonus with the Dodgers but never really delivered for them. They worked with him for five years before giving up and sending him to the Senators. Since then he has been one of the most dangerous sluggers in the game.

A change of scenery often helps a slumping hitter, if for no other reason than that his new manager welcomes him as the good hitter he used to be instead of a guy who's lost his swing. This attitude alone can bring a swing back. The man stops pressing, stops thinking about his swing, and the next thing he knows he's hitting the ball well again.

I suppose it's the thinking that hurts as much as anything. When you have spent most of a professional career swinging properly without thinking about it, then suddenly have to think before swinging, your swing will suffer. I don't know what makes a man lose his swing. All I know is that there have been times when I lost mine and had to work—and think—harder than ever to get it back.

Don't get me wrong about this thinking business. I never heard of a great hitter who isn't thinking about something while standing at the plate. But his thoughts aren't on his swing. He takes that for granted. The thinking he does while he's up there is what kind of a pitch he might see, how this pitcher usually handles him, whether he should try to outguess the pitcher, what the game situation is and what it calls for on his part, and a dozen or so other things. But he doesn't think about his swing. That should be the last thing on his mind.

The one question people ask me most is when to start swinging. I could give a hundred answers because baseball is such a precise game and there are so many possibilities. Furthermore, the ball is coming so fast that I don't have time to get into a debate with myself about when to swing.

However, I can't decide to swing prematurely either. No great hitter stands up at the plate with the idea of hitting the next pitch, no matter where it comes. On the contrary, hundreds have been ruined by just such a decision. That was one of Frank Howard's problems with the Dodgers, and until Ted Williams began managing the Senators, it was a problem for Howard in Washington. Once Williams got him out of the habit, the pitchers had the choice of pitching to him or walking him.

After my 1967 season I had a tendency to get overanxious, swinging simply because I had decided to go for whatever came up. I had lots of trouble in 1968, even though I won the batting championship that year with the lowest winning average—.301— in the game's history. One of my problems was a premature and preconceived swing.

The best time to swing is the very last second. The best hitters are last-second hitters. One of the greatest who ever lived is Henry Aaron of the Braves. Old-time baseball men who have seen many more stars come and go than I have tell me Aaron has the fastest wrists the game has ever known. He can wait until the ball is almost on top of him before committing himself, then snap his bat around so fast he literally takes the ball right out of the catcher's hands.

Williams, DiMaggio, Mantle, Cobb, Ruth, Hornsby—you name the great ones and I'll show you guys who waited until that last second before swinging at a pitch. I try to do that, but don't always succeed. For that matter nobody, not even the superstars of past and present, *always* succeeded. If they did, the record books would be full of .500 hitters. Today a .300 hitter is considered a stickout.

When Williams, the last of the .400 hitters, batted .406 in 1941, he was once asked, "How does it feel to be a .400 hitter?"

"Well," he replied, "if your boss gave you ten jobs to do and you did six of them wrong, how would *you* feel?"

He was kidding, of course, but that really *is* the situation in baseball. The edge is always with the pitcher. Every time you go to bat, the odds are against you. A .300 hitter gets three hits every ten times up. That means he fails seven times. It is almost a rule of thumb that when an outstanding pitcher is in his best form, few batters, if any, will hit him safely.

To say the best time to hit is the very last second doesn't mean that every good hitter can wait that long. That takes a superstar —somebody like Aaron or Williams or DiMaggio, for example. Most of us just aren't that quick with the bat. I know I'm not. While there are times when I can almost pluck the ball out of the catcher's mitt, I get most of my hits—in common with other ordinary mortals—by starting my swing just before that last second.

I keep my eye on the ball, picking it up as soon as possible after it leaves the pitcher's hand, but I don't decide whether or not to swing until it reaches a certain zone—a point perhaps twenty or twenty-five feet in front of me. Remember, the ball is traveling fast, so I don't have all day to make up my mind. I think—but I'm not *positive*—that I actually begin my swing when the ball reaches that zone. The reason I'm not positive is that everything is happening so fast.

Of course I can find out later, when looking at movies of myself, exactly when I began my swing simply by having the camera run slow-motion. Sometimes I start at that zone, sometimes I wait a trifle longer. The longer I wait, the better off I am because the more I see. If I start swinging when the ball reaches my zone, I have to take it for granted I know where the ball will be when my bat reaches the point of contact—assuming I make contact. If I can wait, I don't have to take anything for granted. I can see what the ball is doing, not anticipate what I think it will do.

This takes fantastic eyesight, but I never heard of an outstanding hitter who didn't have that. I have fine eyesight or I would never have become a star or had a dream year like 1967. They used to say that Williams—there's that man again—had the eyesight of six people in a hundred thousand. He himself has pooh-poohed the theory that his great sight made him a great hitter, but there's no question that it helped.

This is why so many good hitters with normally good sight wear glasses or contact lenses—Frank Howard and Richie Allen, for example. By ordinary standards their sight is as good as anybody's, and under ordinary circumstances they don't need glasses. But trying to hit a round ball going ninety miles an hour with a round bat is not an ordinary circumstance.

Several guys in both leagues, either sensitive about their not quite adequate sight or finding glasses awkward, wear contacts. I think every hitter who needs something to beef up his sight would wear them if he could, but many can't adjust to them. One that I remember vividly was Earl Torgeson, who had his best years with the old Boston Braves. He tried several times to wear contacts, but just couldn't get used to them. Torgeson, however, was an exception, because he always wore glasses anyhow.

Another question people ask me is if I ever actually see the ball meet the bat. Sometimes I think I do, but it's probably an illusion. I see the ball right up to that slightest fraction of a second before actual contact between ball and bat is made, but I doubt if I (or anyone) ever sees the actual meeting of the two.

I've asked other ballplayers the same question, and I get pretty much the same answer. Once in a while a guy will quickly say, "Sure I see it." But then I ask him which gives, the ball or the bat, and he can't tell me. I suppose it must be the ball, since that's made of horsehide and the bat is made of wood, but I couldn't prove it by my own experience. As a matter of fact, even pictures are unlikely to give the answer because it happens so fast there's always a slight blur—just enough to keep you from making the distinction.

Once a hitter starts his swing he nearly always must go through with it. You often see somebody appear to begin his swing, then pull back, but if he can do that he hasn't really started. He might be bluffing or he might just be taking his bat off his shoulders, in which case he can hold back. But once that bat starts moving he has committed himself and can't stop it. This is why you sometimes see a good hitter look very bad on a pitch. He probably *thought* he was going to swing and then, too late, decided not to. It's happened to just about everyone I've ever seen in the majors, including me.

It's when the ball reaches the zone I spoke of that I make my decision. If I'm going to swing, I probably start there, and having done that, I can't change. Even if I don't like the pitch and know I will either miss it or hit it poorly, I try to go through with the swing. A half-swing or an arrested one is worse than no swing at all. It's one way to pull a muscle or suffer some other minor but nagging injury that can keep you on the shelf for a week or so.

Fans often wonder why hitters get fooled so often by slow stuff. This too happens to the best of batters. A good pitcher always uses the same windup, if he uses one at all. Before he throws his slow pitch, he does everything exactly as he would if he were coming in with a fast ball or a fast-breaking ball. Watching him, the batter can't tell if the next pitch will be a change until it's halfway to the plate. By then he may have already committed himself.

From what I hear, Warren Spahn probably had the best change of any pitcher in the business. I faced Spahn only a few times—in exhibition games down south—and by then he was beyond his peak. But he was still going, and his best pitch was that slow curve. He must have been one of the few pitchers in the game who used it in clutches. It was so deceptive that when he put it where he wanted to, only luck or a miracle enabled a hitter to get a good piece of it.

I hate slow stuff. Most good hitters do. Everyone I ever talk hitting with prefers a fast ball to anything else. The reason, of course, is that a fast ball provides much of its own power. If you hit it squarely, it might go out of the park. A slow pitch or a breaking ball has to be hit harder to go as far.

Although you might not hit well before going into pro ball, keep swinging if you have that swing. It's best to use a weighted bat, or one with one of those "doughnuts," because the heavier the bat you practice with, the lighter your regular bat will feel when you play. From the time I was eleven or twelve I often swung at nothing. Sometimes I spent two or three hours a day in the middle of winter swinging out in our garage in Bridgehampton. I wanted to be a big-leaguer then, and now that I am one, I want to remain one as long as possible, so I keep on swinging.

The best thing of all is batting practice. I take hours of it. Even after the first game of the 1967 World Series, I went out with a few teammates—Hawk Harrelson, Joy Foy, and George Scott—and took about two hours of batting practice. It's the only way to keep in your groove, or to get into it if you have lost it.

They say the only way to learn to write is to write and keep on writing, provided you have the tools. The same is true about swinging. If you have the tools, the only way to learn to hit is to keep swinging. And that's the only way to keep on hitting, too.

24. *The swing:* Getting set for pitch.

25. Rear view.

26. Starting step as pitch comes in.

27. Step short,
perhaps less than an inch.

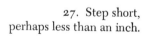

28. Close-up of legs in start of step.

29. First move in taking bat off shoulder.

30. Continuing move to swing—note slight uppercut.

31. Another view of
actual swing.

32. About to make contact.

33. A demonstration of what *not* to do. I have taken my eyes off the ball and am looking at bat. I missed the pitch by a mile.

34. Now I have hit the ball and am beginning follow-through.

35. The full follow-through after hitting the ball. This was a home run to dead center field at Fenway Park in Boston.

36. Completing follow-through after hitting ball.

37. Another view of
follow-through.

38. With follow-through completed, I'm dropping the bat. This was on
that home run, a line drive that went into the stands so fast that it was
there by the time I dropped the bat.

5.

THE STRIKE ZONE

There is nothing easier to define in baseball than the strike zone. All you have to do is look in the book. Under rule 2.00, which is devoted to the definition of terms (listed alphabetically), you will find: "The STRIKE ZONE is that space over home plate which is between *the batter's armpits and the top of his knees* when he assumes his natural stance. The umpire shall determine the strike zone according to the batter's usual stance when he swings at a pitch."

Well, that looks plain enough. Between the armpits and the top of the knees. And, of course, between the two sides and the front and back of home plate. Any kid who plays baseball knows where the strike zone is. And every ballplayer, young or old, amateur or professional, has forgotten at some time or another during his career. Once forgotten, it's the hardest thing in baseball to find.

Why do we all forget? I've got a few ideas, but I'm not sure if they're right. I'm supposed to be a good hitter, but I lose the strike zone every so often. I think one reason is overanxiety. I walk up to the plate, take my stance, start pumping, look at the pitcher—and wait. I can't make a move until the pitcher throws the ball. If he makes me wait too long I step out of the box to make *him* wait, but I can't get away with that too many times before the umpire warns me to stop stalling. Fortunately the same thing is true of the pitcher. Sooner or later he *must* throw the ball. But in the meantime, while I've been waiting and he's been fiddling around the mound, I sometimes have become so eager to swing that I lose the strike zone.

Perhaps this happens because of the angle. When a man takes his stance at the plate, he gets an altogether different view of the strike zone. No matter how long you study the rule book, no matter how sure you are that you know where the strike zone is, the minute you step into the batter's box your angle in relation to it is as different from any other angle as green is from red. If you're not careful, you can get all fouled up. The strike zone, so easy to define, so easy to find from any other angle, suddenly disappears.

It used to disappear sometimes even when it was bigger than it is now. Today's rules give the batter a slightly better break than he had before 1969, when the top of the strike zone was his shoulders and the bottom his knees. They made a big deal out of this rule change, but it hasn't mattered much. The difference between the old rule and the new is too small to give the batter a decisive break.

Now you would think that anybody who can read should know the strike zone, and everybody who has read the official baseball rules certainly knows where it is. But that rule is general. The trick isn't necessarily to know where the *general* strike zone is, but where *your* strike zone is. That line about the batter's natural stance adds to the possible complications.

No two men have exactly the same strike zone any more than they have exactly the same grip or stance or swing. A tall man has a different strike zone from a short one, a heavy man a different strike zone from a light one, a fat man a different strike zone from a thin one, a croucher a different strike zone from a stand-up hitter.

"According to the batter's usual stance . . ."

Who's to decide what his *usual* stance is? What if he changes his
stance? What if he experiments with his stance, trying to find the
most comfortable and effective one? How does the umpire know
what his "usual" stance is? How does anybody? How does the
batter himself know?

If you change your stance you change your strike zone. Some
hitters change their stance in accordance with the pitcher they
face. Every change a batter makes gives him a different strike
zone. This is true no matter how he stands or how often he
changes or in what way. Of all the people involved, he is the one
who should know that strike zone best. Sometimes he's the last
to find out.

Nothing in baseball is more elusive, nothing more controversial,
nothing a worse hazard to a hitter. When you lose the strike zone,
you don't hit the ball properly, your swing is out of line, your
judgment of strikes and balls goes haywire, your strike-out total
rises, and you end up falling into a dismal slump. I know. It happens to me all the time.

There's hardly a hitter in the major leagues it hasn't happened
to. And when he loses the strike zone, he must beat his brains
out to find it again. The only hitter I've ever known who *always*
knew the strike zone was—you guessed it—Ted Williams. I think
he's the only hitter in history who was never known to swing at
a pitch a fraction of an inch off the strike zone.

Opposing ballplayers used to insist that the umpires were inclined to give Williams the best of it on a pitch he let go by. Since
I was never on the same ball club with Williams, I can't say
whether this was true or not. However, I suspect it probably was.
Williams knew the strike zone as well as the umpires did. He took
plenty of called strikes, but most were on the first pitch, which
he rarely swung at. He also often took second called strikes.

But he almost never took a third called strike. If such statistics
are available (which I doubt), I think they would show that
Williams took fewer third called strikes than anyone in the game.

When he had to swing, he swung. And the few times he was ever called out on strikes, he never squawked. He knew he had taken a third strike before the umpire did. I'm told he sometimes started walking away from the plate before the umpire made his call. When Jim Hegan was catching for the Cleveland Indians, he once said he'd rather see Williams up in a clutch situation than Joe DiMaggio. Hegan knew the ball *had* to be in the strike zone to make Williams swing. With Ted this was rule of thumb no matter what the game situation. DiMaggio, on the other hand, considered the game situation, and if it called for a hit he often went for a pitch slightly off the strike zone. That didn't necessarily make a better hitter out of DiMaggio, but it gave the opposition more to worry about. The pitcher knew he could walk Williams by keeping the ball even a trifle out of the strike zone. He couldn't do that with DiMaggio.

Not that DiMaggio was a bad-ball hitter. He knew the strike zone almost as well as Williams did. But if he thought he could get a clutch hit on a pitch out of the strike zone, he would swing and more often than not get his hit.

Williams' argument against swinging at anything even slightly out of the strike zone was that if you started doing it, you might never stop. You would fish farther and farther away until you'd finally be trying to hit bad balls. Therefore, he reasoned, you *must* stick to the strike zone because then you never would be tempted to stray from it.

There have been some good bad-ball hitters. The best was Yogi Berra, who could hit home runs off his ear or golf them from his ankles. Berra was in a class by himself, however. I personally have never seen another consistently good bad-ball hitter. Not that I've never seen guys hit bad balls safely. I've done that myself occasionally. But one of the very first rules of batting is to know the strike zone and never swing at anything that isn't in it.

I wish I could follow that rule to the letter the way Williams did. If nothing else, it would keep me out of some of those terrible slumps I fall into. A man who knows his strike zone and refrains from swinging at anything else has almost got this hitting problem licked. He'll never lick it completely because of that edge good pitchers have over good hitters. Even Williams went into an occasional slump, but his never lasted long because he never lost sight of the strike zone. His troubles weren't usually of his own making anyhow. The average batter goes into a slump because he starts doing something wrong. Most of Williams' slumps weren't slumps at all. He kept on hitting the ball well, but didn't get his hits because too many went right at fielders playing out of position. If they had played where they belonged, Williams might have hit .400 more than once.

Of course every good pitcher knows the strike zone as well as a good hitter does. Spot pitchers—and there aren't many good ones—are more consistently successful than pitchers who depend on fast balls or a repertoire of off-speed and breaking pitches. Everyone used to say Eddie Lopat of the Yankees was great because he was a "junk" pitcher—that is, he threw slow, tantalizing stuff that looked easy to hit but wasn't. But there have been a lot of junk pitchers who never lasted long because all they had was junk. The real secret of a junk pitcher's success is his ability to put the ball where he wants to somewhere in the strike zone, and Lopat was a marvel at it.

Whitey Ford was another great spot pitcher. He knew every fraction of an inch of the strike zone, and where every one of his pitches was going. Of course both he and Lopat were bombed once in a while because they weren't infallible. They had their bad days just as hitters do. When they couldn't put the ball where they wanted to, they were in trouble.

Perhaps the best spot pitcher of all time was Warren Spahn. He studied pitching the way Williams studied hitting. To this day he tells young pitchers, "You've got seventeen inches to play with. Anything you throw within those seventeen inches and between the batter's knees and his armpits is a strike. Take advantage of every fraction of an inch. It's all yours."

Spahn could take advantage of every fraction of an inch. He

knew every pitch in the book, and could put any pitch he threw into some corner of the strike zone whenever he felt like it. So, you say, if the pitcher's knowledge of the strike zone is as good as yours, what good is yours? Perfectly logical question. The answer goes back to the batting averages. The pitcher who knows what he's doing—and no pitcher ever knew better than Spahn—has that natural advantage over the hitter.

This doesn't mean that you, the hitter, just throw in the towel when you face a tough pitcher who knows as much about the strike zone from his angle as you do from yours. But if you don't stick to the strike zone with your swings, you're giving that pitcher an added advantage. He doesn't even have to get the ball over the plate to make you swing.

The big leagues would be full of .300 hitters if everyone remembered the location of the strike zone. That includes me, because I'm just as bad as everyone else. When I lose the strike zone it takes days—sometimes weeks—for me to find it again. The only thing I can do is work harder and longer in batting practice.

It helps if you have somebody—a teammate, a coach, anybody who knows the baseball business—standing behind the cage and telling you if you're swinging at bad balls or not. If I pop a pitch up or foul one off or miss the ball altogether in batting practice, I ask if it would have been a strike if I hadn't swung at it. There's always somebody around to tell me. If somebody's catching, he will. If nobody's in a position to see, I yell down to the pitcher and ask him.

The importance of knowing the strike zone simply can't be overemphasized. Other things being equal—that is, if you're doing everything else right—nothing will get you into a slump faster than losing the location of those little dimensions so clearly defined in the rule book. Yet the big leagues are full of otherwise good hitters who constantly get into trouble trying to hit bad pitches.

Mike Epstein is a good example. He came up with a great reputation as a slugger in the minors, and it certainly was warranted. This guy had all the tools to be a superstar, just as his Washington teammate Frank Howard had. But at Baltimore, Epstein couldn't find the strike zone any more than Howard could with the Dodgers. Both learned it when Ted Williams became their manager. Epstein could still become almost as fine a slugger as Howard if he remembers what Williams, I'm sure, constantly drills into his head.

I once lost the strike zone because of a sly stunt pulled by Eddie Stanky when he managed the White Sox. The night we opened a series in Chicago, Eddie had the groundkeepers line up the batting boxes crookedly. Nobody noticed it when the game began, including our first two hitters. When I came up and checked my stance by tapping the other side of the plate with the end of my bat, I found myself practically facing third base, so I knew something was wrong. I stepped out of the box and squawked to the umpire, who hadn't noticed it either. He ordered the lines fixed, but the damage to me had been done. I was confused all night and didn't get a hit. It took me nearly a week to find the strike zone again.

While the necessity of knowing the strike zone is pretty obvious for hitting purposes, it has another big advantage. If you lay off pitches out of the strike zone you'll get a lot more walks. Any good hitter should draw upwards of a hundred bases on balls a year. The record book has several categories of bases-on-balls leaders down through baseball history. Nearly all those listed are held by superstars—guys like Babe Ruth, Mel Ott, Ted Williams, Eddie Mathews, Jimmie Foxx, and Richie Allen. One year Ruth got 170 passes in 152 games. Williams led the American League in walks a record four straight years and got one hundred or more walks a record six straight years.

The only reason all the walking records aren't held by superstars is that some ballplayers—Stanky in particular—were specialists at drawing walks. Stanky's mark of 148 in 153 games still stands as a National League record. Eddie Joost was a wonder at drawing passes. Of the modern players the best at it are Willie McCovey, Jim Wynn, Richie Allen, and Ron Santo.

All of which means one thing—that these guys knew the strike zone better than anyone else. I've led the league or been up in the top three or four walkers most of the years that I spent in the majors. I usually got the most walks in my best seasons, which means I lost the strike zone the fewest times in those years. The less walks I got, the more often the strike zone disappeared on me.

Learning the strike zone transformed Frank Howard from a dangerous hitter into a superstar. When Williams got him to keep away from bad pitches instead of trying to hit them downtown, his walk total zoomed from 54 in 1968 to 102 in 1969. Williams, who worked as hard trying to keep Epstein from swinging at balls off the strike zone, got Mike up from 48 passes in 1968 to 85 in 1969.

For reasons I shall never understand, pitchers who later treated me with kid gloves pitched to me all through my best season—1967—when I led the league in just about everything except walks. I could see why pitchers were so nice to me in the early part of the season because I had Tony Conigliaro batting in the cleanup spot behind me. Until he was badly hurt when hit by a pitch in August, he was as dangerous a hitter as I—if not more so—therefore the opposition had to pitch to me. But once Tony was out for the season, I never could dope out why they continued to, when they could have pitched around me. I didn't get a hundred walks in 1967.

The pitchers made up for that the next year when they pitched around me all the time. With no Conigliaro behind me—he had to sit out the whole 1968 season—they could afford to walk me, either intentionally or by not giving me anything decent to hit. We tried half a dozen good hitters in the cleanup spot, but nobody could handle the job as well as Tony. I often got disgusted and tried to hit pitches I knew were off the strike zone, but that only made matters worse. Because of the lack of a cleanup hitter, I walked 119 times in 1968, a year which was not nearly as good for me as 1967. Even in 1969, when I had a comparatively poor season except for home runs, I walked over one hundred times.

Here then is one of the big advantages of knowing the strike zone and losing it as rarely as possible: you get a lot more walks. Only with a Conigliaro or someone comparable to him as a hitter behind you will you see many good pitches in the strike zone. When Conigliaro made his miraculous comeback in 1969, the pitchers figured Tony hadn't come all the way back—and they were probably right—so they continued to give me more walks. I ended up with 101 for the season.

When Conigliaro came all the way back in 1970, my own situation improved. We had plenty of good hitters on our 1970 club —Petrocelli, Andrews, Smith, Scott, Moses, most of our regulars, in fact—but none was as good a cleanup man as Conigliaro at his best. This was why we had problems in 1968 and 1969 which we didn't have in 1970. When Conigliaro was traded at the end of the 1970 season, I could only hope we had someone capable of replacing him to follow me in the batting order.

Although I don't entirely agree with Ted Williams in his refusal to swing at *anything* off the strike zone, I'm with him a hundred per cent on his insistence that learning it and never losing it is a prime secret of any batter's success. That's why I worked so hard to learn the strike zone and why I work so hard to this day to maintain my awareness of it. And that's why I can't stress its importance too much.

6.

SLUMPS

Nobody knows exactly what causes slumps, and everybody has different theories on how to break them. Although I guess I'm one of the better hitters in baseball, I'm an expert on slumps. I get into too many for a good hitter, and they last too long. There are a million ways to fall into a slump, and I think I have found most of them.

Aside from conventional reasons—changing your stance without noticing it, breaking some fundamental rule of batting, facing a succession of pitchers especially tough for you, losing the strike zone, swinging too hard, taking your eye off the ball —there are also a few unconventional reasons for slumps. Maybe you're working too hard and need a rest. Maybe a trifling but nagging injury has put you into a bad habit to compensate for it, and the habit lasts longer than the injury. Maybe worry about personal problems is wrecking your concentration. Or maybe you're just getting bad breaks, hitting the ball well but into the wrong places.

A slight injury probably cost Jimmie Foxx the one chance he ever had of breaking Babe Ruth's old home run record of 60.

Foxx had 50 on Labor Day in 1932, when he hurt his wrist sliding into a base. The wrist healed quickly enough, but having to favor it a couple of days threw Foxx's timing off. He hit only eight more homers during the whole month of September.

Some of baseball's greatest hitters got into terrible slumps. Ty Cobb once went 0 for 32. Rogers Hornsby set a strike-out record in the 1929 World Series. Ted Williams had only five hits —one a bunt down the unprotected third base line—in the 1946 series. Gil Hodges didn't get a hit in the 1952 series. He played all seven games and actually had all of Brooklyn praying for him, but nothing helped. Even when he hit the ball hard, it went right at somebody. The same thing once happened to Bing Miller. He was batting over .400 the first month of one season, when his luck ran out. Everything he hit went right at someone, and as his average fizzled his temper flared. He finally blew sky high, lost confidence in himself, and had a bad year.

I suppose there are almost as many theories on how to break a slump as there are ballplayers who have them. Personally I try to follow the advice originally given by Ty Cobb and still given by Ted Williams—just try to hit the ball back at the pitcher. This keeps you from overswinging, helps you get back into your normal groove, and makes you keep your eye on the ball.

Ordinarily, of course, you won't actually hit the pitcher. You're just using him as a target. He's the nearest ballplayer in front of you and the easiest man to aim at. The ball you hit trying to hit him might go anywhere. It doesn't matter. The point is to try to make contact with your bat and let nature take its course. I know some ballplayers who hit that way all the time. They're not power hitters, but they don't pretend to be. All they're trying to do is get a hit.

When you're a power hitter—as I'm supposed to be—you're at something of a disadvantage. You feel an obligation to the ball club which most of your teammates don't have. They depend on you for the long ball. If you're in the proper groove you'll hit your share. But if you're out of your groove you won't hit anything for a while.

The situation changed somewhat on our ball club when Rico Petrocelli became a power hitter and Tony Conigliaro came back. Almost everyone who plays regularly for us has the ability to hit one out of the park occasionally, but you can't call them power hitters with the exception of Petrocelli and George Scott. Scott's trouble is similar to my own. When we hit, we hit well and far. When we don't hit, we go into bad slumps.

I think the cause of most of my slumps is overswinging. I didn't really become a power hitter until 1967, when I had 44 home runs. That year I deliberately tried to hit home runs after a spring training during which Ted Williams, who was still a part-time batting coach for us, showed me some of the tricks of the trade. He made me change my stance slightly and swivel faster on my hips. By bringing my bat around quickly, I had already learned to wait on a pitch, although, as I have pointed out before, my wrists aren't quite strong enough to permit me to take the ball out of the catcher's hands.

As I look back on it today, I realize that Williams' lessons, although very effective when they worked, failed to help me much when they didn't. Since I'm a streak hitter, my slumps nearly always follow hot streaks. I don't fall into a slump gradually or without realizing I'm in one. I go a couple of weeks doing everything right, then suddenly I do something wrong and the slump begins.

I think—although I'm never sure—that my very success is what leads to eventual disaster. As I hit the ball more often and harder, I have a tendency to forget that I'm doing it with my hands and wrists, and start trying for even more power by swinging harder. Pretty soon I'm overswinging. A slump actually is using too much body. When I try to muscle the ball instead of letting my wrists do the work, I move my body too much. This leads to pulling my head out instead of keeping it in the same position, which I must do when I'm hitting properly.

I hold my bat too high, get overanxious, and can't wait to go to the plate and swing away. After a while I develop a hitch in my swing which causes me to undercut too much. When things get really tough I start going after bad pitches. At this point I'm at the peak—or maybe I should say the bottom—of my slump.

In my early years with the Red Sox I practically panicked when I went into a slump. Now, however, as soon as I know I'm heading in the wrong direction, I go to the television studio and study pictures of myself made while I was hitting well. This eventually gets me out of it, although I never know how long it will take. Sometimes I learn what I'm doing wrong in a couple of hours, sometimes it takes several days.

Learning what I'm doing wrong is one thing. Correcting it is something else again. I usually can break a slump in about a week, but I have gone two or three weeks before really getting out of one. When that happens, I spend more time in the studio because I know that I'm probably doing more than one thing wrong. Obviously, the more mistakes I make at the plate, the longer it will take for me to get back into the right groove.

This is not a unique situation. Every good hitter gets into trouble somewhere along the line. If he has access to pictures of himself, he can break out of a slump fairly quickly. If he hasn't, he must depend on teammates or his hitting coach or sometimes even an opposing player to show him what he's doing wrong. The hitting fraternity is like the pitching fraternity. We're all in the same business, we belong to a mutual admiration society, and if we can help each other with suggestions without hurting our own ball club, we sometimes do.

Not during a game, mind you. That's not the time to discuss problems with the opposition. On the contrary, when a good hitter is in a slump, the other club takes full advantage of it. The more mistakes you make, the better off that club is. The suggestions that might help never are made on the field. They come in casual conversation with a friend on another team. But once the ball game starts, it's war. A good hitting catcher, for example, will never say, "You're lifting your head" or "You're using too much body." He'll tell his pitcher that, but not you.

In 1969, when Ted Williams managed the Senators for the first time, he helped so many opposing hitters who asked him for suggestions that some of the men on his own ball club objected. Giving advice came as natural to Williams as breathing. Hitting was his favorite subject. In his first year as a manager anyone who asked him for advice got some, regardless of whom he played for. Later, when Williams realized he might be hurting his own club, he became stingier with useful suggestions. But I doubt if he'll ever stop giving them altogether. He likes to talk hitting too much to turn his back on any ballpayer who brings the subject up to him.

I don't have nearly as much trouble learning what I'm doing wrong as making corrections. It's one thing to sit on the bench discussing your problems and making up your mind to correct them. It's quite another to go to the plate and, facing an opposing pitcher instead of a batting-practice pitcher, carry out all the instructions you have been so busy giving yourself.

Something happens to slumping hitters when they get into a ball game. They crouch in the on-deck circle watching the pitcher, trying to concentrate on just how to handle him while swearing to themselves that they're going to correct those mistakes that caused all the trouble. But when a man in a slump arrives at the plate, all his good resolutions go out the window. Don't ask me why. They just do, that's all.

When I get up there during a slump, I forget everything but the distant fences, which I try to reach with every swing. I fish for bad pitches, swing too soon, move my head all over the place, and become one of the world's great pop-up or strikeout artists. This is a tough thing to lick because it's mental as well as physical. When I'm hitting well, I never think of the fences. I just try to hit the ball. Then I'll belt one out of the park or into the stands every so often.

The old-time ballplayers had some interesting slump-breaking theories. Although Ty Cobb later advised just trying to hit the pitcher, he first used to get out of slumps by bunting. Since he was one of the best bunters who ever lived, and had the speed to go with it, he was pretty successful stopping slumps that way. First he would bunt conventionally, then he'd push a bunt or two, then start drag-bunting, and finally start swinging. It worked with him because he had all the necessary tools for getting on base by bunting. It wouldn't work for most of us, though I have tried it. Tony Conigliaro was the most successful guy on our club at bunting his way out of slumps.

Lefty O'Doul had an unusual but successful way of killing slumps. After learning who the opposing pitcher was going to be that day, he would get the teammate whose style was most similar to pitch batting practice to him in the morning. If that didn't work, he just went out and played a round of golf.

Johnny Mize, a great hitter, aimed for the pitcher. He once succeeded too well. Ewell Blackwell, a long, lean guy with a smoking fast ball, was pitching for the Reds when Mize, then with the Giants, was in a bad slump. Blackwell threw a fast ball which Mize rifled right back at Blackwell's head. Blackwell jumped away so fast that he swallowed his tobacco. The incident served a double purpose. It got Mize out of his slump and Blackwell out of the tobacco-chewing habit. He never took another chaw.

Jimmie Foxx ignored slumps. He had them but refused to think about them, on the pretty sound theory that the more you thought the more you worried, and the more you worried the worse the slump. Foxx insisted that slumps were mental bogeymen. He just kept swinging, figuring that sooner or later everything would be all right, and sooner or later everything was.

When Connie Mack managed the Philadelphia Athletics, he rested slumping hitters—all but Foxx, who never wanted a rest and never recognized a slump. Spending a couple of days on the bench isn't a bad idea. It's a lot more tiring to play when

you're in a slump than when you're hitting well. The very fact
that you *are* hitting acts as a stimulant and psychs you up to a
point where every ball game is a pleasure. I've rarely seen a
hot hitter get tired in the middle of a good streak. It's only when
he's in a slump that he gets so exhausted that the game becomes a chore.

I've always felt that one of the real hallmarks of a great
manager is his ability to pull a good hitter out of a slump.
Managers get blamed for everything and are almost the first to
be fired when things go wrong. A team collapse is rarely the
manager's fault. The decisions he makes are mostly cut and
dried. Any intelligent baseball fan can run a ball club when it's
going well. All he has to do is play the percentages, and every
good fan knows those—how to platoon lefties and righties, when
to bunt, when to take a pitch, and so on. Somebody—it seems
to me it was either Birdie Tebbetts or Leo Durocher—once
said 95 per cent of a team's victories would be won without
the manager, and that the only difference a manager can make
is in the other five per cent. Well five per cent of a season's
schedule is somewhere around eight games. In division play
that can be the difference between first place and fifth or sixth.

If the team's star is in a slump and the manager pulls him
out of it, the guy will start hitting, the club will win more
games, and the manager will have earned his salary. From what
I hear, although I never saw him in action, Billy Southworth,
who managed the Braves to their last pennant in Boston, was
a marvel at getting a slumping ballplayer to start hitting again.
Long before it was customary to make movies of good hitters
for use when they began having trouble, Southworth helped his
slumping players by memory. He learned every batting charac-
teristic of every ballplayer he ever had, and recognized at once
the slightest change.

Today neither a manager nor anyone else on a ball club
needs a memory like that because movies serve the purpose even
better. However, I think there are cases when a manager or a

batting coach could help a young ballplayer in a slump by watching the pictures with him and pointing out flaws the player himself might miss. I watch my own movies either alone or with a friend or two because I know my own batting characteristics well enough to recognize mistakes that show up when I go into a slump.

As far as I know, the first ballplayer to use movies for help in breaking slumps was Ted Kluszewski. When he was playing for the Reds, his wife took dozens of pictures of him at the plate. When he stopped hitting, they ran the movies in slow motion on a home projector.

Although slumps are nearly always caused by some fundamental mistake, luck plays a big part in them, just as it does in all phases of baseball. When you're riding high you get all kinds of hits—long hits, leg hits, line hits, Texas leaguers, infield nubbers, everything. When you don't get a good piece of the ball, it still often drops in safely. I couldn't count the number of cheap hits I've had when I was going well. Three fielders would converge on a pop fly and none of them would touch it. A ball would hit a pebble and bounce over an infielder's head. An outfielder would misjudge a fly ball and play it into a double or triple.

These are bonuses that come when you're hot. But the payoff comes with your solid hits. When I'm hot I get plenty of those, all the way from line singles to home runs. I get many more real hits than fluke hits when I'm swinging properly. It's just that my luck runs good because everything else goes well.

It works just the opposite when I'm slumping. My luck goes bad with the decline of my hitting. When three fielders converge on a pop fly, two back off while the third man catches it. The ball that hits the infield pebble moves smoothly into the infielder's hands and he easily throws me out. The misjudging outfielder becomes a ball hawk, moving in the right direction with the crack of the bat and making a simple catch of a routine fly ball. And even when I hit the ball well, some guy makes a spectacular play, or a solid drive is caught by a fielder who doesn't have to move a step.

In the early part of the 1970 season, Mike Andrews, then of our club, normally a .265 or .270 hitter, went into a nose dive at the plate. The poor guy couldn't do anything right. When he dropped to .183, went something like 0 for 21, and was obviously pressing, Manager Eddie Kasko gave him a few days' rest.

"When you're going bad," Andrews said, "you swing at bad pitches. And when your luck is also going bad, you hit them."

He came up one night in the sixth inning of a game against the Tigers, with runners on first and second, and one out. Andrews reached for an outside pitch and hit a soft liner to the pitcher, who converted it into a double play.

"That's what I mean," Mike said later. "That pitch was so far outside I should have missed it by a foot and it would have only been a strike. But the way my luck was going, I got my bat on it and hit into a double play that got the Tigers out of the inning."

That same week, with two balls and no strikes on him, Andrews made up his mind to swing at the next pitch, which he was sure would be over the plate.

"I decided to swing," he said, "and the ball came in over my head. I was committed, so I swung away. Instead of missing it by a mile, I got a little piece of it and popped it up."

Normally Mike wouldn't have swung at either of those pitches, both of which were far out of the strike zone. But the guy was in such a horrible slump that he would have done anything to get a hit. That included fishing for bad pitches, a common fault for anyone who can't beg, borrow, or steal a base hit.

Al Kaline once told me about a monster slump he had in 1956, which was before my time in the majors.

"Before I got out of it," he said, "I was pressing, anxious, not waiting for my pitch, swinging too hard, and going for the fences. I think it was nearly a month before I got back into my regular groove. A rest gave me a chance to work things out in my mind, and finally I was all right."

In those days Kaline was the guts of the ball club. He didn't want a rest but knew he needed one. I guess he was on the bench for about three days, and he hated every minute of it because the ball club had to have his bat to get anywhere. I feel the same way when I take a rest. The Red Sox do need my bat—working properly—and I know I'm not doing them any good on the bench. But sometimes it's the only answer.

It's odd how much less a ball game takes out of you when you're hitting than when you're not. The feeling is much like the difference between playing for a winner or a loser. While ballplayers on winning teams get so psyched up that they are never really tired, ballplayers on losing clubs are always exhausted. They drag themselves out to the park, hang around the clubhouse in sullen silence, and instead of thinking positive, wonder what's going to beat them this time. Since they go out expecting to lose, they usually do, and when the game is over they're dead tired.

Victories are stimulating, defeats debilitating. Hitting streaks are wonderful, slumps terrible. I never know when a slump is coming, or what I'll have to do to get out of it. I guess the only real way to handle them is to stay out of them in the first place.

7.
STRATEGY

In the days of the dead ball, strategy was an integral part of baseball. The old-timers, unable to hit many home runs, got on base and scored runs more with their heads than their bats. Then along came Babe Ruth, the ball was livened up, and suddenly the most effective strategy of all was the home run. It's still the most effective strategy. There's no substitute for it. It's the ultimate, the perfect solution to all batting problems.

Slugging teams like the old Yankees, the old Athletics, the Giants of the forties, the Braves of the late fifties, the Reds of the early sixties, even the current Orioles, never had to think much about strategy. When teams like those were going well, the only strategy was to get as many guys as possible on base so more runs would score when somebody hit a homer.

In most of those years baseball was a slugger's game. When the rule makers began putting in changes that tended to favor the pitcher, the pendulum swung the other way. Today's Orioles notwithstanding, the rules still favor the pitcher. There was a time when a pitcher would end up in the minors if he couldn't go the distance consistently. Today he can last five innings without losing his status as a starter, because bull pens are filled with relief specialists capable of going anywhere from one to five innings as effectively as he can. Because of that and bigger and more uniform ball parks, night baseball, the slider, long-distance travel, and radical time changes between the two coasts, baseball became a pitcher's game by the mid-sixties. The rule makers have since come up with a few minor changes, shrinking the strike zone and lowering the pitcher's mound a little. These have been some help to hitters, but not enough. It's still a pitcher's game.

So the strategy of the home run, while as effective as ever when it works, can't be depended on any more. Heavy-footed slugging ball clubs, made up of muscle men who can't run, slide, or bunt, no longer dominate the game. Hitters again have to use their heads as well as their bats to get on base and to score runs. Brute strength won't do the job any more. You have to think while you're up at the plate, and you have to keep on thinking after you hit the ball, when you drop your bat, while you're on base, and indeed until the moment you score, if you do.

Not that you would expect a Frank Howard or a Harmon Killebrew or Boog Powell to bunt when you're a run or two behind and have men on base late in a ball game. Nor any other long-ball hitter, regardless of size or strength, including myself. Any man capable of hitting a lot of home runs might hit one at any time. If it happens to be near the end of a game that would otherwise be lost, so much the better.

When I had that amazing year in 1967, late in close games I went to the plate absolutely positive that I'd either hit one out of the park or come up with a base hit that could mean the ball game. This wasn't strategy, it was confidence—the kind of confidence you acquire when you're going well and your team is in the thick of the pennant race. I have no idea exactly how many games I either tied or won in the ninth or in an extra inning in 1967, either with homers or lesser hits. I do know that I had never had such confidence before, and up to now haven't had since. It was just one of those years that probably comes once in a lifetime.

While strategy in general is popularly accepted as the manager's job, players often have to consider split-second strategic possibilities, both at the plate and on the bases. Just how much a player can use his own judgment is up to the manager. Some managers, notably John McGraw and later managers who played and learned from him, would not let anyone make a decision for himself. To them baseball was a chess game and the players simply pawns to be moved around as they saw fit. But most managers—including practically all the ones for whom I have played in Boston—give their players plenty of opportunity to think for themselves.

For example, few managers order the hit-and-run. In most cases the batter makes that decision, usually with a man on first and less than two out. A good hitter knows the general patterns the pitchers use on him. Often he has every reason to look for a fast ball in the strike zone—in fact, any kind of pitch in the strike zone. Although he will usually have to take orders from the bench on whether to take or swing at a cripple (a three balls and no strikes or three and one count), he can put on a hit-and-run under any other conditions. Sometimes the manager lets him decide even in a cripple situation. I've often been given the green light to swing whenever I wanted to, and so have many other good hitters in both big leagues.

The hit-and-run is just that. When the batter gives the sign for it, the runner will go with the pitch because if the batter hits safely, he has a good chance to make it to third, since he's almost at second by the time the ball is hit. If the ball goes to right field or right center, he'd have to be a truck horse not to reach third on a hit-and-run. But if it's a hard-hit ball to left, he might have to stop at second, because of the short distance of the throw from left field to third base.

One of the most overworked and exaggerated expressions in

baseball is "hitting behind the runner." In the past, with a runner on first and less than two out, the question of whether the shortstop or the second baseman would cover second was practically automatic. With a right-handed batter up, the second baseman covered because the hitter was more likely to hit toward the left side of the infield, so it wasn't considered safe for the shortstop to leave his normal position. The opposite was true with a left-hander at bat, making it necessary for the second baseman to stay where he was while the shortstop ran over to cover second.

All that is changed today. With a man on first and less than two out, who's at bat doesn't determine which of the middle infielders will cover second. There are too many other things now taken into consideration—the type of batter, the kind of pitch, the speed of the base runner. A spray hitter usually hits the pitch rather than trying to pull, as a slugger might. A good spot pitcher can make any hitter, even one who usually pulls the ball, hit it in any direction he wants him to.

For example, an outside pitch to a left-handed hitter will usually go to the left because outside pitches are the hardest to pull. Naturally a good hitter will pull one once in a while, but the odds are that he won't. Since even a left-handed hitter figures to hit an outside pitch to left, it would be suicide for the shortstop to move out of position to cover second base. The ball is likely to go right through the hole he leaves.

The opposite is true of a right-handed hitter, who will normally hit an outside pitch to right, so it won't necessarily make sense for the second baseman to leave his normal position to cover second. Both the shortstop and the second baseman know what the pitcher will throw. One or the other is usually in charge of making the final decision who will cover second. With men on base—especially on first—and less than two out, you will always see one of the middle infielders cover his face with his glove and give a signal to the other. It's usually a very simple signal, like opening or closing his mouth, which keys the man who receives it as to which should cover.

In the meantime neither the batter nor the base runner really knows. But since it's the batter who must decide whether or not he intends to swing, the base runner will never give a hit-and-run sign. While the batter may try to place the ball, he won't hit "behind the runner" purposely. If he does, it will be plain dumb luck, not strategy.

The one big advantage of hitting behind the runner is that it gives the runner a better chance to reach third from first. But under present-day baseball conditions, hitting behind the runner can no longer be done purposely. In the old days you knew where the infield hole would be. Today you have to guess.

In the last analysis the guy who decides whether the shortstop or the second baseman should cover second is the catcher or, if he is calling pitches from the bench, the manager.

There are some great hit-and-run batters in our league. We had two of the best in Reggie Smith and Mike Andrews, both of whom hit well to all fields. Andrews was traded to the White Sox after the 1970 season. Apart from the Red Sox, Danny Cater is the one who first comes to my mind. Although a right-handed batter, he can hit as well to right as to left. When I'm in my groove, I do a fairly good job, but I'm more of a straight-away hitter than anything. I pull when I can, but if it's impossible, I'm more likely to hit to center. As a left-handed batter I rarely try to hit to left on purpose except occasionally at Fenway Park, which has a short left field fence that doesn't break out sharply.

While the batter controls a hit-and-run situation, the base runner controls the run-and-hit. When he gives the signal for it, it really means that he will try to steal. He wants the batter to know this if for no other reason than to make sure he swings at the next pitch, no matter where it is, to try to distract the catcher. If the batter gets a base hit, the runner has a good chance to make it all the way to third. If it's a bad pitch, he must swing anyhow, and perhaps the runner will succeed in stealing.

This strategy backfires when the hitter fouls one off. Every fan who has seen a foul ball ruin a stolen base wonders why the batter swung at all. He swung because he had to. The run-and-hit was on.

We all try to put on a hit-and-run from time to time when the base runner is at second. Here again it's the batter's decision unless the manager's policy is to give all those signals himself. In a way it's easier to hit and run with a man on second than on first. You know the middle men—the shortstop and the second baseman—will stay in their normal positions because neither has to cover third. That means you won't get robbed if you hit one down the middle, something that often happens when one or the other covers second with a man on first and less than two out. And if your hit-and-run succeeds with a guy on second, he'll almost surely score, no matter where your base hit goes.

You also have a better chance to get a leg hit—a nubber to the infield that you can beat out—if you hit and run with a man on second. The third baseman is stuck with a Hobson's choice. If he sees the runner coming down from second base, he has to cover third. If you top a ball and hit it slowly down the third base line, he should field it, but he can't do that and cover third, too. Even if it's short enough for the pitcher or the catcher to field it, he probably will have to throw to first, not third. Then, although you won't get your hit, you will at least have advanced the runner.

I don't often put on a hit-and-run with a man on second because seeing him running affects my concentration on the pitcher, and I sometimes lose sight of the ball. Fans like to watch everybody run when there are two out, the bases are full, and the count on the batter is three and two. If I'm up under those conditions, I tell the man on second not to run. If he just hovers off the bag he won't bother me, and if I hit safely it won't much matter whether he's close to second or on his way to third. He'll score anyhow.

Except to try to beat it out with the bases empty, hitters rarely bunt without orders from the bench. I've seldom bunted with men on base under any other conditions. Not that I've never bunted at all, or wouldn't now if ordered to. But I don't get the bunt sign unless there's nobody out, a man on first, and we're one run behind in a late inning. Then we all have to do what we can to move the guy up, because he represents the tying run.

One of the prettiest plays to watch is a successful squeeze, a bunt to bring a man home from third. There are two kinds of squeeze bunts, the safety and the suicide. In both cases they're put on almost invariably by the manager's orders. In a safety squeeze the man on third takes a normal lead but doesn't start running hard until the hitter has laid the bunt down. If he misses the ball altogether, the runner has time to get back to third.

But on a suicide squeeze the runner goes with the pitch, and then the hitter *has* to make contact with the ball. If he misses it, the baserunner usually looks foolish. Unless he's very fast, he'll be a dead duck at the plate. And if the hitter pops it up, the runner will be easily doubled up.

The ball park has a lot to do with hitting strategy. As new stadiums are built, there is less and less variation. They all have about the same seating capacities and dimensions. The distances along the foul line are usually the same in each direction, but it means little even when they're short, because the stands break out so sharply. Fenway Park is a good example. It's actually shorter along the right field line (302 feet) than along the left (315 feet). But how many times is a home run hit to right exactly on the foul line in Boston? I'll bet I haven't seen an average of one a year since 1961, when I first joined the Red Sox. The break is so sharp that the average distance from the plate to right is 382 feet.

But that's about the only resemblance Fenway Park has to most of the new stadiums. We have a ball park that was built in 1912 and remodeled a couple of times in the thirties. The last important change was to shorten right field by putting bull pens in front of the bleachers, largely to accommodate Ted Williams. It also accommodated every other long-hitting left-handed batter in the American League, including me.

Fenway Park is famous as a right-hander's paradise, not because it's only 315 feet from the plate to the left field fence along the foul line, but because the break is so gradual from left to center that a good hitter can bounce one off the fence or hit one over it with a high fly ball that goes anywhere from 315 to 350 feet. Although one of the deepest in the American League, dead center—420 feet away—is a healthy but not impossible drive.

I suppose it comes under the general head of batting strategy that some left-handed power hitters might go to left to take advantage of the Boston fence. I have occasionally done it, but only if the pitch is right. Early in the 1970 season I became the sixth man in history to hit one over the center field bleachers in Boston. It was off Dennis Higgins of Cleveland, under almost perfect conditions. He was a right-hander; his pitch—a belt-high fast ball between the middle and the outside of the plate—was perfect; my swing was perfect; and my wrists were perfect. Only the weather was less than perfect.

It was a cold day with a fairly stiff cross wind which probably would have kept the ball from leaving the park or even from going into the stands, if it had been a high fly. But I hit this one on a line right into the teeth of the wind, and it was going so fast that the wind didn't affect it. I would have liked to see what would have happened if there had been no wind at all, or better still a tail wind.

I knew by the sound of bat meeting ball that this would be one of the best-hit smashes of my baseball career. When you hit a fast ball on the nose the way I hit that one, you know it's gone before you start running toward first. Usually, even when you hit one well, you feel a little vibration—no pain or sting, just vibration—in your hands. This time I didn't feel anything. I don't remember ever having felt just that way on hitting a ball.

In the first inning of the same game I hit one off Dean Chance which I thought would go over the fence in left center, but it was too high and the wind kept it in the ball park. I can tell by the feeling when I hit the ball solidly. Everything clicks well. But I always had *some* feeling in my hands, as I did when I hit the ball off Chance. The other one, which jumped off my bat like a shot, was the first that left me with no feeling at all, as though I were a well-functioning machine, as inanimate as the ball itself.

Yet the smash wasn't all accidental. In order to take better advantage of the Fenway wall, I had been working hard all spring on hitting long drives to the left of center. I'm not a bit sure the one off Higgins actually was the longest I ever hit. I belted one in Oakland early in the 1970 season that might have gone farther, and in 1969 I hit the bottom facing of the third deck in Yankee Stadium. In neither case, however, did I have that complete absence of feeling in my hands.

Incidentally, I am the smallest man ever to hit one over the Fenway Park center field bleachers. The others were Jimmie Foxx, Hank Greenberg, Mickey Mantle, Bill Skowron, and Don Lenhardt, who was our batting coach when I hit the ball off Higgins. He saw it go out from his post in the first base coaching box. All those guys, including Lenhardt, were big strong muscle men. At six feet and 185 pounds I'm a midget compared to them.

While that short fence in left makes Fenway Park a south-paw pitcher's nightmare, it has its disadvantages for a hitter. I've seen many good righties ruined by it because it looks so close that they constantly overswing trying to reach it. Most of them forget two important points—that the fence, although close and breaking out very gradually, is unusually high, and that pitchers keep the ball away from them as much as possible.

When a right-handed batter gets a pitch easy to pull at Fenway Park, it's always by mistake. No pitcher, left or right, will purposely throw a hittable inside pitch to a right-handed batter.

The fence really is easy to hit if you stay loose, because you don't necessarily have to pull to hit it. I've seen good, bad, and indifferent batters hit or clear it in left center. Jose Santiago, a pitcher hardly noted for his slugging ability, belted a home run there off no less a star than Bob Gibson of the Cardinals in the 1967 World Series. Santiago didn't pull that ball. It was a fast ball which he happened to hit squarely, and it went into the screen nearer center field than left.

Our most successful right-handed batters—guys like Rico Petrocelli and Reggie Smith when he bats right (he's a switcher) —have learned not to think about the left field fence when they come to the plate. As a result they all hit or clear it fairly consistently. But visiting right-handers—hard-hitting rookies and veterans alike—don't think about much of anything else while they're at bat. Some go nuts, muscling, overswinging, swinging too soon, doing everything wrong as they try to reach that fence. We probably have as many pop flies and topped rollers hit by good visiting batters as any club in the league.

A lot of good hitters go into a slump after a Fenway Park series. They concentrate so much on trying to reach our short left field fence that they lose the rhythm of their swing, and it takes a while for them to get it back. Only really great right-handed hitters who know the park well—the best example I can think of is Joe DiMaggio—don't let the fence affect their normal swing. This of course is no problem for a left-handed batter. He might try to go with an outside fast ball occasionally, but he doesn't change his fundamental hitting style. I've seen many left-handers hit the fence and sometimes clear it, but I know of nobody except Ted Williams in his later years who deliberately hit one over it. I'm told Williams was hitting more and more to left as he got older, to break the radical shift opposing fielders used against him.

Part of batting strategy is learning when to try to stretch a hit from a single to a double or from a double to a triple. While on my way to first base after hitting a ball, I always think of the possibility of stretching it. If it's a hot line drive bouncing right into an outfielder's hands—which would be an easy throw to second or to the cutoff man—I know I'll just make the turn and go back to first. But if the outfielder has to run after the ball, I'll go for two because I have the speed and he has to get into position before throwing. And of course if one or two out-fielders box the ball around, I'll try for two. Or if the fielder has a notoriously poor arm. Or if, taking it for granted I won't try to stretch, he lobs the ball to the cutoff man.

The hitter can make all those decisions for himself while going from first to second. But he often needs help from the third base coach in deciding whether to try to stretch an obvious double into a triple. When he hits to dead right field, he can't see the ball without turning around after he passes second. A fast man like Tony Oliva may get away with committing him-self even after losing sight of the ball. But most base runners watch the coach, who will wave them back to second if there's any doubt of their making it to third. If the coach lets the runner come, he gives him the sign whether to slide or not.

The coach may also decide if he can go all the way for an inside-the-park home run. The last one I hit was early in the 1968 season. All I remember is that it was hard work and I was dead tired after sliding across the plate. It's easier on the legs to hit the ball out of the park. That's the kind I like best. And there's no better batting strategy in baseball.

8.

SWITCH-HITTING

If I had my life to live over, I'd have been a switch-hitter by the time I was old enough for Little League. Anyone who goes into professional baseball knowing how to bat from only one side of the plate is at a distinct disadvantage. It's fine to say that as a left-handed batter I save a step running to first after hitting the ball, but I wish I could hit right-handed, too. Then I could see any kind of pitching as clearly as I see left-handers.

My son Mike, who is approaching Little League age, will be a switch-hitter if he decides on baseball as a career. I've already started teaching him to switch. I don't know how good he'll be —he's too young to tell yet—and of course I don't know if he'll want to make a career of baseball. But I do know that if he decides to try, he'll be a switcher, because I think anyone with a big league batting potential should switch.

Very few good switch-hitters make the change successfully after they become professionals. The only one I can think of off-hand is Maury Wills. A natural right-hander, he had such a tough time with right-handed pitchers that his manager at

Spokane, Bobby Bragan, made him switch. With his speed, his quickness in learning to switch, and his general intelligence, Wills got back into the big leagues and has been there ever since.

Wills, however, was an outstanding exception to a general rule—if you don't learn to switch as a kid, you never will. I could easily have become a switcher when I was young. As far back as I can remember, another boy and I used to play a batting game with a tennis ball in our back yard. He was a Yankee fan and I loved the Red Sox. We went right down the line-ups of the two teams, each not only taking the part of all the regulars but batting as they batted.

I was pretty small then—eight or nine maybe—so my memory of how well I did when it was my turn to bat right is very dim. But I do know I swung often from the right side, and if I had kept it up, I think I would have been good at it. But my father, a good semi-pro ballplayer who knew the game well, eventually made me stick to the left side of the plate because I was a natural left-handed hitter.

At the time my father was right. In those days—the forties—the advantage of switching was not nearly as obvious as it is today. Although always a pressure game requiring intense concentration, baseball was easier on everyone. The slider alone has made it tougher for hitters. A pitch that comes up looking like a fast ball, spinning like a curve, and moving in different ways (depending on the guy who throws it) is tough to hit. When I was young, the slider either wasn't invented yet or was simply not in general use. A pitcher could make it to the majors with three basic pitches—a fast ball, a curve, and a change. Now he needs a slider, too. And believe me, a slider is much harder to spot and to hit than any of the others.

There are other differences that have changed baseball's situation in general. When my father was working with me, the big leagues had only sixteen teams. Expansion hadn't begun and the two major leagues combined were concentrated between Boston in the east and St. Louis in the west. The schedule was shorter, the clubs traveled by train instead of plane, and the individual series in each city were longer. With both the Giants and Dodgers in Greater New York, a National League team could spend eight or nine days on the road without changing hotels. Night baseball was just beginning to be common but wasn't the chore it is today, because you never had to rush for a plane at midnight to get to the next town, which may be three thousand miles away.

Taking all these factors into consideration, the pressures of baseball were concentrated on the field. Off it there weren't any pressures. Ballplayers were always rested, always ready to play, and they almost always found playing itself a pleasure.

A switcher was a rarity, because hitters didn't need that extra advantage that switching offers. The sharper you are, the less difference it makes what the pitcher is. In the forties a consistent hitter was always sharp enough to hit any pitcher. Even if he occasionally had trouble with men pitching from the same side he batted from, he rarely had to worry about being yanked. As a rule there wasn't anyone on the bench who could outhit him. He could ride out a slump without having to think about some guy replacing him on any sort of permanent basis.

But now the slumping hitter either gets platooned or benched. Some hitters are platooned all the time anyhow, depending on the pitcher. If a left-hander starts for the opposition, the left-handed hitter with a regular platooning partner knows he'll be on the bench when the ball game begins. Even in batting practice he takes his cuts only against right-handers, while the right-handed batter works only against southpaws.

The left-handed batter plays more often because there are more right-handed than left-handed pitchers. Yet there are more natural right-handed than left-handed hitters. If a right-handed batter is a fringe hitter—good enough to make it to the majors but not good enough to hit any kind of pitching—he spends half his life regretting his inability to bat left-handed.

By then, of course, it's too late to learn. There aren't that many Maury Willses around.

When I was growing up, there were very few really good switchers in the big leagues. The best was Red Schoendienst, who although he never won a batting title was often close. Jim Russell is the only other one I remember. He played for several National League teams and was one of the few men ever to hit homers from each side of the plate in the same game twice.

The best old-time switcher was Frank Frisch. In eighteen years in the majors he had a lifetime batting average of .316. But it wasn't as important to be a switcher in his day as it is now. Relief pitching was mostly confined to second-raters who couldn't make the regular rotation, and platooning was never heard of.

When I'm in my groove I don't care what the pitcher is. But if I'm in a slump, it makes a big difference. As a left-handed hitter I have no alternative but to do the best I can against any pitcher I face. But southpaws give me trouble when I'm not hitting. If I were a switcher, I'm sure I could get out of slumps much faster than I do.

The greatest switcher who ever lived was Mickey Mantle. Mantle started switching as soon as he was old enough to hold a bat in his hands. As a kid he had a rare opportunity to learn because both his father and grandfather were semi-pro ballplayers, and one threw right-handed and the other left. Long before he was old enough for any type of organized amateur ball, Mantle could switch with almost equal ability. He was the only switcher ever to lead the American League in batting.

The best switchers today are Pete Rose in the National League (who has led it a few times in batting) and Reggie Smith, Don Buford, and Roy White in the American. Rose, White, and Buford are not power hitters, but they hit well for average. Smith is the longest-hitting switcher in baseball today. Having played on the same club with him since 1967, I can assure you this guy is well on his way to becoming a superstar.

Rose, White, and Buford are stickouts, but I'll take Reggie over any of them. He can hit the long ball both left-handed and right-handed, and has hit homers from each side in two different ball games. I think he'll do that a good many more times before he's through, but I don't suppose even he will ever match Mantle's record of switching home runs in ten games.

There are quite a few other switchers in the majors, but none in a class with Rose, Smith, White, or Buford. I guess the best-known collection of switchers on the same team were the four Dodger infielders in the 1965 and 1966 World Series. Wes Parker, Jim Lefebvre, Maury Wills, and Jim Gilliam were all switchers. That was one of the main reasons the Dodgers won those two pennants in a row. It was impossible for the opposition to gain anything by using either a southpaw or a right-hander against them.

Besides White, the Yankees have two other regulars, Horace Clarke and Gene Michael, who switch. All these men are better hitters as switchers than they would be if they could bat from only one side of the plate.

Although I myself am used to it, I find locker room visitors often staring at Reggie Smith while he takes practice swings. First he'll swing half a dozen times right-handed, then turn and do the same thing left-handed. His swings used to be quite different. He chopped down more from the left than the right. However, the longer he played, the more similar his swings became. He now chops equally well from both sides.

A man like Reggie can wreck the opposition's strategy in clutch situations. A manager will often bring in a pitcher to pitch to one man, then replace him with another pitcher if the next batter bats from the other side of the plate. But you can't do that with Smith because he simply steps across the plate when a new pitcher steps in.

Come to think of it, I don't remember a single instance in which a relief pitcher was brought in especially to face Smith.

The rest of us on the Red Sox see it happen often because it does make sense. Even when I'm hitting well, it would be percentage baseball to send a southpaw in just to face me late in a close game. As I have said, it really doesn't matter what sort of pitcher I face while I'm in my groove, but it is a fact that I can't watch a left-hander's moves as well as a right-hander's.

This is another big advantage to being a switch-hitter. He has an unobstructed view of whomever he faces. When I say an unobstructed view, I mean that a man like Smitty can watch every motion of any pitcher's throwing arm. He sees it all the time.

But when I face a left-hander, there is a point where I lose sight of his arm. This is a blind spot very much like the one you get as a car is about to pass you on the road. You know he's there because you have seen him coming in your rear-view mirror. But for a fraction of a second, just as he is about to come abreast of you, you can't see him at all. You pick him up again only when he actually passes you.

The same thing happens when a batter faces a pitcher who works from the same side he bats from. I can see a left-hander take only part of his windup, if he has one, or all of his stretch if there are men on bases. But I lose sight of his arm at a certain point. If he's one of those guys who are all arms and legs —like Warren Spahn, for example—I sometimes don't pick his arm up again at all until he releases the ball.

This is one cause of a hitter's trouble facing a pitcher on the same side as himself. Sometimes you pick up the ball too late to see what kind of pitch it is. At other times, even when you know, you have to remember if that pitch runs in or goes away from you when it reaches the plate. If the pitcher has several speeds at which he throws the same pitch—and most of the best pitchers do—you're in even worse trouble because of that blind spot.

But when I face a right-hander, there isn't any blind spot. I can see every move he makes without changing my stance or moving my head. And any time you can see all of a pitcher's motion, you'll never lose sight of his arm or the ball. This is true of all hitters, good and bad, left-handed and right. That's why the lefty batter always has a little edge when facing a right-hander, as does a right-handed batter when facing a lefty pitcher.

Switch-hitters don't have those problems. They can always see everything they have to see to be most effective as hitters. As Reggie Smith often points out, the angle of his vision never changes—it simply mirrors itself. He's always facing a pitcher who throws from the opposite side from where he hits. And he always sees everything, including the pitcher's arm as he winds up and the split second when he releases the ball.

Some baseball men say switch-hitting is a sign of weakness, but I think they're wrong. To me it's a sign of strength, but only if you grow up with it. Once again I refer back to Maury Wills. Switching *was* a sign of weakness with him. He couldn't hit right-handers at all when Bragan made him switch. After Wills learned to bat left-handed, he handled right-handers as well as southpaws. In fact he became a better right-handed batter than before because he no longer had to worry about right-handed pitchers.

Hopelessly bad-hitting pitchers, of whom there are several in both leagues, sometimes switch simply because they have nothing to lose. I can't think of any offhand, but I know a few right-handed batting pitchers who go over to the left just to bunt. Bunting isn't so tough that it can't be learned from either side of the plate. And in an entire line-up the one man who should know how to bunt is the pitcher, unless of course he happens to be a good hitter.

Believe it or not, Rico Petrocelli had such a tough time when he first came to the majors that, in desperation, he tried switching from right to left. It didn't work and, as it turned out, wasn't necessary. Rico is now one of baseball's real power hitters. He bats right and always will. His problem when he first came up was exaggerated by his lack of confidence in himself. He had been a good hitter in the minors. As soon as he learned he could hit just as well in the majors, he stopped trying to switch. In his case, switching at that stage of his career would definitely have been a sign of weakness.

But if a boy starts young—perhaps even when he's as far advanced as high school—he can make a better hitter of himself by learning to switch, and that would be a sign of strength. Good major league switchers like Smith, Rose, White, and Buford insist it *is* a sign of strength, and I agree with them.

There's only one pitfall I can think of which would make it inadvisable to switch. If you find it impossible after giving it a try, forget it. There are plenty of good right-handed hitters who probably never could hit left, and vice versa. If you are one of those, you'll find out soon enough. Don't fight it. If you do, you might be in danger of hurting your ability to hit well from your natural side. And to hit well from only one side of the plate is far, far better than not to hit well at all.

9.

JUDGING PITCHES

When Ted Williams insisted that the toughest job in sports is hitting a baseball, he said a mouthful. As a kid I loved all sports—baseball, basketball, football, track, you name it. I set a Long Island schoolboy record for basketball scoring which, if I'm not mistaken, still stands. I may not have been the best, but I wasn't the worst schoolboy football quarterback when I played at Bridgehampton. I still fool around with golf and tennis, and I've even boxed a little. Nothing is like hitting a baseball. That's hard enough in school and in the minors. In the majors it's an art.

Since no smart schoolboy pitcher tries to fool around with breaking stuff until he gets to be a junior or senior, I never saw much of it as a kid. The best schoolboy pitchers are the fastest. Anyone who can hit a fast ball should do well up to about the age of sixteen. After that, he will begin to see breaking pitches, and the older he gets and the more he plays, the more he will see.

This is what makes big league hitting so hard. By the time a pitcher reaches the top, he's likely to have an assortment of breaking pitches. If he's a stickout, he can throw them at various speeds. And as I have mentioned before, no pitcher has a complete repertoire without four basic pitches—a fast ball, a curve, a change, and a slider.

Here and there a pitcher gets by without a good fast ball. If he has one, it's a great asset, but he can manage without it if his control is perfect and his assortment of breaking pitches wide, and if he can throw them at different spots and different speeds. These are the "junk" pitchers. I'd rather face the best fast-ball pitcher in the business than a guy who throws nothing but well-controlled breaking stuff that never goes right over the plate, yet stays in the strike zone when the pitcher wants it to.

I doubt if there was ever a tougher pitcher to hit than Hoyt Wilhelm when he got his knuckler over the plate. Even at the age of forty-seven he was perhaps the best one-inning relief pitcher in the business. Believe me, nothing pleased me more than to see him go to the National League—the Braves—in the winter between the 1969 and 1970 seasons. When he got that knuckler over the plate, nobody could be sure of hitting it. It took plain old-fashioned dumb luck.

When Wilhelm was in our league, he was the only pitcher who could make me change my stance. I used to move away from the plate, because his knuckler usually broke down and in on me. I could get a piece of it once in a while, and I had some hits off his knuckler, though no home runs that I remember.

Tony Conigliaro found Wilhelm the most mystifying pitcher he had ever faced when Tony broke in with us in 1964 as a nineteen-year-old kid. However, as Conigliaro often pointed out, Wilhelm was one of the easiest pitchers in the league to hit when he couldn't get his knuckler over the plate, because he didn't have much of anything else. I think Tony belted a couple of homers off him, and I may have myself, but they weren't off knucklers. They were Wilhelm's version of fast balls. He knew they could be hit but sometimes used them for their surprise value. He fooled a lot of hitters with them, but not Conigliaro. When Tony just about gave up trying to hit Wilhelm's knuckler, he watched for the fast ball. On the few occasions that he ever saw it, he creamed it.

With Wilhelm gone, the only two knuckle-ball pitchers left in our league are Wilbur Wood and Eddie Fisher. I haven't seen much of Fisher, who spent most of his career in the National League, but Wood has been almost as tough for me as Wilhelm. He wasn't a knuckle-ball pitcher when he first broke into the majors with us, and he slipped back into the minors. There he began fooling around with the knuckler and became good enough at it to get a shot with the Pirates. However, he hadn't really mastered the knuckler yet, and went back down after a year or two. Then the White Sox picked him up, and Wilhelm taught him to perfect the pitch. Although Wood's knuckler wasn't quite as effective as Wilhelm's, it improved every year. Furthermore, since he's young enough to be Wilhelm's son, he'll probably get better as he goes along and should have a long and successful career.

I didn't change my stance when facing Wood because his knuckler usually broke down and away from me. Although I choked my bat more than usual (as I did against Wilhelm), I stood as close to the plate as I always do. Even though Wood's knuckler wasn't as baffling as Wilhelm's, it was good enough to give a hitter fits. And Wood had better stuff to fall back on than Wilhelm when his knuckler didn't catch the plate.

My experience with Phil Niekro, now probably the best knuckle-ball pitcher in baseball, was very limited because I saw him only in spring training exhibition games. Niekro won twenty-three games for Atlanta in 1969, so he must be as good as Wilhelm in his prime. As with all good knuckle-ball pitchers, the secret of Niekro's success was his control. When he got his knuckler over the plate nobody could hit him very hard.

It's impossible to judge exactly how a knuckle ball comes in.

This depends on the pitcher and how well he happens to control it on a given day. It moves slowly and without much spin, so you can practically count the stitches. When it reaches the plate it might go in any direction—down, up, in, away, anywhere. Even catchers don't know what to expect. That's why they use oversized mitts when a knuckler pitcher is on the mound.

Actually you don't really have to study a knuckler to recognize one. When a pitcher has one good enough to throw most of the time, everybody knows it quickly enough, and you watch for it automatically when you face him. I can't remember a knuckleball pitcher with a better pitch in his repertoire. When Wilhelm was younger and could go nine innings, he never had to throw anything else. As an Oriole pitcher he once no-hit the Yankees using nothing but knucklers the whole way.

Another specialist who gives us all plenty of trouble is Mike Cuellar of the Orioles. He saved his own sagging career by developing a screwball, which is really a reverse curve. Cuellar is a left-hander whose screwball breaks in on a left-handed batter where his curve breaks away. Unlike a knuckler, which a pitcher can use exclusively when he can control it, a screwball won't live by itself. Not many pitchers throw it, but those who do need a pretty good assortment of other stuff. It can be hit, which is more than you can say about a good knuckler.

When I face Cuellar, I look for a fast ball or a curve as often as a screwball. Sometimes I can spot the screwball by Cuellar's wrist motion. If I miss that, I can usually pick it up by the spin when it is about twenty feet in front of me. Since it spins in the opposite direction from the curve, I know it will break toward me and probably jam me if it is in the strike zone.

I guess the greatest screwball pitchers in baseball history were Carl Hubbell and Warren Spahn. Hubbell depended very heavily on it. Spahn used it as a money pitch from time to time, but he had such a wide assortment of stuff that it was just another good pitch for him. Fortunately for hitters, there aren't many screwball pitchers. The pitch is very hard on the arm, especially the elbow. To this day both Hubbell and Spahn have crooked left elbows.

One of the best pitchers I ever faced was Whitey Ford, who was a wonder at throwing a batter off stride. He had a wide variety of pitches, several changes of speed, and excellent control, and was almost impossible to beat at Yankee Stadium. We had a lot better luck with him in Fenway Park, where in common with so many southpaws he had trouble because of our left field fence. If I'm not mistaken, he didn't face us more than half a dozen times in Boston during the last few years of his career. Although he beat us twice as many times as we beat him, most of his wins against us were in New York.

While off-speed, offbeat pitchers are often successful, the real stars are the guys with great fast balls. Just because I happen to prefer fast balls over anything else doesn't mean I enjoy facing guys like Denny McLain or Sam McDowell. Both have marvelous fast balls. Although McLain has the more spectacular records, I think McDowell is even faster and in some ways a better pitcher.

McLain rarely tries anything fancy. About ninety per cent of his pitches are fast balls. He can overpower a guy with his speed. For variation he occasionally throws a sinker and once in a while changes speed. But that fast ball is his stock in trade. Even when you know it's coming you can't do much about it.

McDowell, on the other hand, not only has as good a fast ball as McLain—maybe better—but also the fastest slider in the American League. The best sliders are the fastest. We have had some really good slider pitchers in our league, but nobody has one like McDowell's. His comes in so fast that you often can't pick up the spin until it's right on top of you.

Ray Culp of our club has a very good slider. When Milt Pappas was at his peak, his slider was as good as anyone's. So was Earl Wilson's. Of the younger pitchers in our league I think Andy

Messersmith of California, Jim Hardin of Baltimore, and Dick Bosnan of Washington have the best sliders.

A good slider will usually come in straight and go down and away at the last minute. If it's thrown fast enough, it's hard to pick up the spin—which is like a curve—under the best conditions, and almost impossible at night. This is why it's so effective. Unlike other conventional pitches such as fast balls, curves, and changes, you often don't recognize it until it's too late.

If you catch the spin, you still don't know if it's a fast curve or a slider. When in doubt, I guess. If the pitcher is known to have a good slider, I'll move up on it, trying to hit far enough in front of the plate to make contact before it breaks. If I guess right and am in my groove, I might hit it out of the ball park. If I guess wrong, I'll look like a bum because a curve starts moving before a slider does. Sometimes you can hit one if you get far enough in front of it. The ideal curve for a batter is one that hangs. Then it doesn't break at all—a pitcher's misfortune and a hitter's delight.

The best way to tell a fast ball is to watch for the white of the ball. One guy's fast ball may hop, another's may sink, but everybody's has the same spin. As the ball turns, you don't see much of the red stitching. The white predominates so completely that once you get used to picking up the spin, you will know it's a fast ball.

That doesn't necessarily mean you can hit it. If it did, guys like McLain and McDowell wouldn't last a season. Knowing what the pitch is—and most good hitters can tell after they've been around long enough—helps you only when you can adjust your swing to it. A really good fast ball rarely comes in right over the plate. It may be flat—on a straight line from pitcher to plate—but it will almost always do something.

Mickey Lolich's fast ball sinks and moves in on a left-hander. Mel Stottlemyre has one of the best sinkers in the league. It goes down and away. We once had a fine young pitcher named

Don Schwall, whose natural fast ball was really a sinker. He had one great year, then seemed to lose his knack, and the Red Sox finally traded him to Pittsburgh. He had a tough time there because National League umpires were more inclined to call balls on low pitches than American Leaguers were, and Schwall never did do much over there.

A right-handed pitcher's slider will spiral away from a left-handed hitter and toward a right-handed hitter, and vice versa. Curves act the same way. Both have forward spins, in contrast to a fast ball, which has a backspin.

Most change-ups have little or no spin at all. Although they look easy enough to hit, they aren't, largely because a hitter seldom is ready for one. You have to be set for a fast ball most of the time because if you prepare for anything else and get a fast ball, you're dead. You just don't have time to readjust. Occasionally you might get set for a change, but only when you're guessing. And the only time it pays is when you guess right.

The only real exception to the rule of setting yourself for a fast ball is when you know the pitcher never throws one in a given situation. So there are times when I look for a breaking pitch, but I don't remember ever being set for a change. When facing a really good sinker-ball pitcher like Stottlemyre, a right-hander, I crowd the plate because his sinker moves away from a left-handed batter. I do just the opposite with Lolich, a southpaw. His sinker comes down and in to me.

Knucklers, palm balls, fork balls, all slow pitches, can be adjusted to but not necessarily hit. Very few pitchers use a fork ball because you hold it between your first and second fingers, and not many guys can get their fingers far enough apart to grip a baseball that way. Roy Face, the best of the recent fork-ball pitchers, must have had a big space to start with between the first and second fingers of his right hand. After all those years throwing fork balls, that space is huge and probably permanent.

While many hitters don't recommend guessing, I think it does me more good than harm. Every pitcher has his money pitch, and it's a pretty good bet that he will throw it in the clutch. Of course this isn't a hundred per cent true. For example, I have been fooled by Stottlemyre when he didn't throw his sinker in a tough spot, and by McLain, who sometimes comes in with his slider after throwing practically nothing but fast balls all night.

Bob Gibson of the Cardinals gave me a terrible time in the 1967 World Series. Since he was a great competitor with one of the game's best fast balls, I expected him to try to overpower me. Instead he threw me nothing but breaking pitches. He shut me out the first time I faced him, but I got two hits off him the next time he pitched, and one in the last game. The only way I did it was by looking for his curve, something I seldom do. He might have stopped me altogether with a fast ball here and there because, being set for a curve, I wouldn't have been able to adjust to a fast ball quickly enough.

What you can or can't hit is no secret to any pitcher. Even when you're set for the pitch you get, you won't necessarily hit it safely. Earl Wilson got me on sliders, and almost always threw me one in the clutches. I knew it, I looked for it, I was set for it, and he knew all that. Yet he still threw sliders at me in tough spots, and I still couldn't hit them.

This of course is what I mean when I say that knowing the pitch is only half the battle. The pay-off is in hitting it safely. It does me no good, for example, to know I'm going to get a fast ball from McLain, if I can't hit it. He throws it most of the time even when he knows I am looking for it, and most of the time I have no better luck with him than anyone else does.

Every pitcher has the right to try to brush you back, although that doesn't give him a license to kill. When a brush-back pitch is thrown purposely it's nearly always a fast ball, fairly easy to get away from. I never get upset at a pitcher who throws close because I know he's trying to move me away from the plate. But when somebody throws the ball behind me, I blow my stack.

Any time an experienced pitcher throws the ball in back of you, he's really trying to hit you, not just brush you back. The only exceptions are rookies, who are sometimes so wild they themselves don't know where the ball is going.

Even when the ball seems to be coming at you, you should try to pick up the spin, because it might be a curve that will swerve over the plate. But when you see nothing but white, you know it won't hook away from you. It's a fast ball that will hit you if you don't get out of the way or fall flat.

I must have been down ten times during the first month of the 1968 season. Almost every pitcher I faced constantly brushed me back, and some fired the ball right at me. Actually very few threw behind me, although it happened a couple of times. The only way to beat brush-back strategy is not to let it affect your normal stance. Even after a brush-back pitch I always stand in at the plate just as if it hadn't happened.

Getting away for a brush-back pitch is really a matter of reflexes. The minute you see what it is, your brain tells you to get out of the way, and you do. Once in a great while, as in the case of Tony Conigliaro in 1967, you might freeze and the ball will hit you, sometimes with disastrous results.

There are specific times to expect a pitch to brush you back. One is the first pitch thrown at you after the guy ahead of you has hit a home run. Another is if you crowd the plate too much, especially with men on base. And a third is if you're in a hitting streak. Under any conditions there's nothing to be afraid of. Your reflexes will usually keep you from getting hit.

One thing you always have to remember is that the pitcher rarely wants to hurt you. All he wants is to make you move far enough away from the plate to give you trouble reaching the outside corner of the strike zone with your bat, because that's where his next pitch is most likely to go. If he makes you gun-shy, you're playing right into his hands. Fear is the natural enemy of all hitters. Don't let it get you.

10.
PRACTICE AND CONDITIONING

The most important commodity an athlete has is his body, and his most important job is to keep it in shape. If your body goes bad, you go bad. The only way you can function is to treat it properly, and that means work—hard work—both in and out of season.

Perhaps I should say work and luck, for luck plays a big part in the life of a professional ballplayer. One injury can nullify the best efforts of a whole year, not only because of the injury itself but because it may get you out of shape. There are times when you can work in spite of an injury. If a man hurts an arm or a shoulder, he can still run to keep his legs in shape. A man with a leg injury can still take exercises that preserve the muscle tone in the upper part of his body. The only injuries which can stop you from working at all are those which keep you bed-ridden or on crutches.

Anybody who goes through a long major league career without an injury serious enough to shelve him more than a week or two at a time is very lucky indeed. Since coming to the major leagues in 1961, I have had good breaks. Except for 1965, when a kidney ailment put me in the hospital for a while, I have never played less than 148 games in any one season. Even in 1965 I played in 133 games. I was in 160 or more games in four different seasons through 1970, and I have every hope of maintaining that pace for some years to come.

Because I keep in shape, I'm not as prone to injury as I might be. Obviously I've been lucky, too. I could always break a bone crashing into a fence for a fly ball, or sliding into a base, or falling while going after a Texas leaguer. Avoiding injuries of that kind is strictly a matter of luck. You can't go all out in baseball and not risk injury.

Or, like Tony Conigliaro, I could freeze at the plate and get hit in the face or head with a fast ball. That too is a matter of luck. No matter how often you have been at bat or how confident you are that you won't be seriously hurt by a pitch, you never know when you might be unable to move away from one. Almost everyone who has suffered a bad injury while batting couldn't get out of the way because some hypnotic force immobilized him—in other words, he froze. I don't recall ever having had it happen to me, but I know it could. It can happen to anyone who must depend completely on his reflexes to keep from being hit.

Except for the month or so immediately following the end of the season, when I am fully relaxed, I try to keep in shape all the year around. This is nothing new with me. It started when I was a kid, and I've kept it up ever since. I have always been conscious of my body. Anyone with professional athletic ambitions has to be, especially when he approaches thirty. It's comparatively easy to stay in shape up to that time. But after twenty-eight or so, you must work increasingly hard every year if you intend to continue playing ball.

By then you have been around and know what to do. But good bodybuilding begins in childhood. It's all right to say that every young boy is active, but the sooner his action takes some direction and the sooner he decides to specialize in one sport the better. Much as I enjoyed all sports, my first choice was always baseball. Everything I did, even as a kid, was with that in mind. The fact that my dad was a semi-pro ballplayer helped a lot. He knew the game well enough to teach me fundamentals, and he knew enough about conditioning to help me as soon as I was old enough to understand.

Some boys are driven off a sport because their fathers force it on them. My father never forced anything on me. He made it plain that he'd rather have me play ball than do anything else, but he didn't make me work at baseball. I did that on my own. All my dad did was play ball with me, answer questions (never volunteering information unless I asked for it), and help me with the kind of exercises best suited for a budding baseball player.

I reacted well because I wanted to, not because I had to. If I hadn't wanted to play ball, I wouldn't have worked as hard as I did when I was young, and I certainly wouldn't have kept it up when I got older. My dad never forbade me to play any other sport and never forced special exercises on me. He played for and managed a remarkable ball club, made up almost exclusively of both sides of my family. In those days the whole tip of Long Island was crazy about baseball. Practically every town within a radius of fifty miles had a semi-pro team, and groups of towns formed leagues. We had two teams in Bridgehampton, the Blue Sox and my dad's White Eagles. Even our local league had so many teams it had to be divided into two sections. Competition was keen and the league championship meant something. I can't remember a Sunday when my grandfather or my mother or some other relative didn't take my brother Rich and me to see my dad play ball.

One of my earliest ambitions was to play for the White Eagles myself. Almost everything I did was geared to baseball. For years I didn't miss a day swinging a weighted bat. Even in the middle of winter I walked through the snow to our unheated garage before supper to swing and swing and swing. Nobody drove me. I did it on my own.

When I was in grade school, a friend of my dad's who lived a couple of doors from us and played for the Blue Sox, used to come over regularly to pitch tennis balls at me. I swung at them with a truncated bat, cut down almost to the trade-mark. Dad's friend, who threw hard, would start forty feet away, then come closer and closer until he was only twenty-five feet away. From that distance I had to bring the little bat around fast to hit the ball. It was great for my wrists.

When there was anyone to play with me—Rich, Dad, a friend, whoever happened to be around—we went to an empty lot across the street and somebody pitched to me while others shagged. One of my uncles rigged up a special gadget which I used when I wanted to practice alone. I put a ball on top of some rubber hosing attached to the outside of a stationary iron pipe driven into the ground. I could adjust the hose by moving it up and down and securing it with screws drilled through it and the pipe. The ball had a hole through the middle, into which was inserted a piece of wire attached to about two hundred feet of line. I could swing at any height I wanted to and after I hit it reel the ball in by the line.

I played catch, hit fungoes, fielded grounders, threw longer and longer distances as I got bigger, played ball wherever there was a game, and swung and swung and swung. I played in grade school, Little League, the Babe Ruth League, and with the American Legion juniors. I played every position at one time or another—pitcher, catcher, infield, and outfield. I wasn't a long-ball hitter, but I hit consistently. Even when too small to hit the ball hard, I had good averages, usually well over .400. All the swinging and exercise, combined with my natural growth, made me stronger as I got bigger. One year in high school I hit .650 and had a string of fifteen straight hits.

I was the youngest player in the semi-pro league—fourteen years old—when I played center field for the White Eagles. By then some of my uncles were sick of baseball and had quit, and

Dad often had to round up other relatives and friends to get a team together. He did it right up to the time I left home for Notre Dame, where I went for a year and a half. With all his concentration on my baseball, my dad was determined that I acquire a college education and never let me forget it. Even after I signed a Red Sox farm contract, I continued to go to school, finally graduating from Merrimack College, not far from my home in the Boston suburb of Lynnfield.

Every winter I worked out somewhere, trying to get myself into shape for spring training. I usually went with other ballplayers in the Boston area, all of us working together, swinging, playing pepper games and pickup, running, throwing, and doing calisthenics. Except for one spring when I started working out too late and put on weight, I reported every year to spring training almost in shape to play.

During the season I work hard to stay in shape. When in a slump I take extra batting practice. I run in the outfield, spending at least half an hour shagging flies. On game days I hold a hard rubber block in each hand, squeezing rhythmically and counting to myself. I squeeze three hundred times with both hands, holding the blocks tight, sometimes pausing for thirty-five seconds. On off days or when a game is rained out, I'll squeeze those blocks with both hands anywhere from five hundred to six hundred times, holding them as tightly as I can for additional 35-second pauses.

This exercise keeps my hands and wrists and arms strong, gives me the feeling of being strong, helps me cut down on over swinging and using too much body in my swing. Then I have less tendency to try to muscle the ball instead of bringing the bat around with my wrists.

The winter before the 1967 season I met a gnome of a man named Gene Berde, who runs a health club at the Colonial Inn in Lynnfield. A former Hungarian Olympic boxing coach, he introduced me to a brand-new regimen of exercise. Although he is more than twice my age, thirty-five pounds lighter and six inches shorter than I, he is about ten times as strong. When he showed me how he did it, I agreed to try his exercises.

They weren't easy. He had me working with wall pulleys; running a treadmill; stretching on a wall ladder; riding a stationary bicycle; skipping rope; tossing a medicine ball; doing high kicks, knee bends, push-ups, arm stretches, backward and forward somersaults; and finishing up with sixty-yard sprints.

I reported to the Red Sox in the best shape of my life and had the greatest year of my life as we won the pennant.

As Gene Berde showed me, it's not easy to stay in shape. Many a time I couldn't stand the sight of that little man and his little gymnasium, which looked like a chamber of horrors to me. I once got fed up and didn't see him all winter, and had one of the worst seasons of my life. Now I'll stick with the guy as long as he'll have me. He makes me work my brains out, but every minute of agony pays off when the baseball season begins.

Not everyone has a Gene Berde to turn to. But everyone can go to a gym or work under a trainer's supervision or even work out at home. If you want to be a big league ballplayer in the summer, that's the price you have to pay in winter. I can't think of a better investment.